The Church Looks at Family Life

THE
CHURCH LOOKS
AT FAMILY
LIFE

Evelyn Millis Duvall
David R. Mace
Paul Popenoe

BROADMAN PRESS

Nashville, Tennessee

DEWEY DECIMAL CLASSIFICATION: 301.42
Library of Congress catalog card number: 64–21162
Printed in the United States of America
5.AL64KSP

Foreword

The home, in the divine plan, has three basic functions—procreation, nurture, and companionship. "Be fruitful and multiply" accents the first; "thou shalt teach these things diligently to thy children" emphasizes the second; "for this cause shall a man . . . cleave to his wife" suggests the third The degree to which homes today succeed or fail in performing these basic tasks runs as a unifying concern through the twelve messages of this book.

That concern prevailed too in all of the sessions of the Southern Baptist Conference on Family Life, where these messages were originally delivered. This significant family life conference brought together responsible representative Southern Baptists to look at the continuing family crisis and its challenge to Christians, both personally and in relation to congregational and denominational responsibility. The aim of the conference was to secure involvement in a united effort to meet constructively the family crisis of our times.

The addresses on preparation for marriage, family life, and special home problems, which are published herein, gave new insights into the nature of the family crisis. It was realized that neither divorce, nor desertion, nor internal family conflict, nor juvenile delinquency get to the heart of the family problem. These are but symptoms. Basically, the problem is in the degree of failure of the home to function as God intended it to, to

v

bring healthy children into the world, to train them for mature responsibility, and to provide mutual affection to all members of the family. Why the home fails to function as a home, and why the degree of that failure has been on the increase is a long-time development due to many factors. The point of great anxiety expressed in the conference and reflected in this book is that a serious crisis is upon us, a home crisis that demands our most serious attention.

Every Christian is concerned about the home, both personally and in the activities of his church and in the organized institutional work of his denomination. The church in all of its work responds to the family challenge—in Bible teaching, in missionary education, in leadership training. Every one has a stake in family life—every agency, every institution, every responsible Christian worker. But too often what is everybody's business is nobody's business. Universality of concern and of responsibility can be both a weakness and a strength. This occasioned the need for a family life conference—to bring about definite personal involvement in relation to ongoing responsibility. That too is the underlying purpose in the publication of these messages from the conference.

Frankly, we need a revolution in our program of Christian education in our churches. Too long we have thought of education by church organizations as a complete entity, without the enlistment of an older agency to which God first gave the command to teach. Too long we have delayed thinking of these church organizations as means through which to train the strongest ally of the church—the Christian home, and the parents to whom God has given the responsibility of bringing up the children in the way they should go. We are looking and longing for the time when the church and the home will join hands in cordial co-operation in a mutual task. The work of the church must in the future be planned to bring about that co-operation and to prepare its members in their homes to engage with the church in the endeavor divinely committed to both.

JOE W. BURTON

Contents

1

Facts and Fictions
About Marriage

Through thirty-five years of listening to young people, I have collected literally hundreds of thousands of questions that young people ask. From time to time I analyze the most recent five-year batch of questions, usually running around twenty-five thousand or more, to find out what these teenagers are asking about love, courtship, and marriage. I am finding great differences as the years roll on. Today's youngsters are asking quite different questions than were asked even twenty years ago. One of the most frequent kinds of questions I find today is the one that begins: Is it true that . . . ? Our young people realize that they have picked up a good many half-truths, a great many fictions, and a lot of the folklore along with some facts that are sound. Therefore, my writing reflects young people's interest in trying to get things straight.

We are the most scientific society in history; yet we live in a prescientific era largely dominated by superstition, taboo, fiction, and folklore about love, marriage, men, women, and family life. Here is a roll call of ten of the areas in which there still is a great deal of confusion and fictitious folklore.

1. One of our confusions still is that "opposites attract," in spite of the fact that to the present date there have been more than 167 studies all pointing to the other direction. Research finds that young people tend to find others like themselves in family background, in religious faith, in race, in social-economic

background. They tend to fall in love with persons like themselves. Overwhelmingly they tend to marry according to the
principle of homogamy—the tendency of persons to marry
persons like themselves. This is not to say that there is no such
thing as mixed marriage, nor that mixed marriage is not on the
increase. Both of those things are true. But the overwhelming
tendency among our young people is to marry persons like
themselves.

2. "Out of all the world," the folklore goes, "there is one
predestined mate, and when the two meet they know it." And,
"each individual chooses one person from out of all the millions
available." The fact is that is nonsense. The studies very
conclusively show that our young people have access only to a
limited number of eligibles. They get really well acquainted
with even a smaller number. Each individual young person
probably knows, even in the most active courtship period, not
more than a half-dozen persons well enough to choose a marriage
partner. Furthermore, we find from the studies that Dr. Jessie
Bernard has done in remarriage and that Dr. William Goode
has done on divorce, that actually any one of us who is fairly well
adjusted, who has learned to love, who has learned to be a
human in the finest sense, could probably marry almost any
other well-adjusted, loving, mature person like ourselves and do
a pretty good job at marriage.

The old idea that if a girl was a good girl and stayed home on
Saturday night and washed her hair and was kind to her
grandmother, that a knight in shining armor would come riding
out of the West on a white charger (or in a red convertible in
more recent days) is just nonsense. The mate selection process is
limited by (1) propinquity and (2) congeniality, and it is an
active selective process about which young people themselves
need to become far more aware. They can't count on magic.
They can't count on the miracle of sudden attraction.

3. "Love is all that matters," so the folklore goes, and the
evidence says, "Nonsense." There are a great many other factors
that are important for the success, even the happiness, of

marriage: (1) becoming individually competent, able to assume the responsibilities of one's own role as husband or as wife; (2) becoming aware of what to expect; (3) learning how to live with differences. Many, many other things are quite as important as love. This is not to say that love is not important in marriage. I would be the last one on earth to say that. My husband and I, celebrating our thirty-fifth anniversary recently, looked back at our own honeymoon and wondered what we were so excited about then, because such wonderful development and growth has taken place in our lives and love through the years.

4. You often hear the statement, "Marriage tends to be taken very lightly today." The impression is that the average young couple getting married today has the feeling almost of crossing their fingers as they say to themselves and possibly to each other, "If this doesn't work out, we can always get a divorce." And the evidence says, "Nonsense." I personally have never met a young person who took marriage that lightly. Our nationwide studies among young people, as well as among adults, show conclusively that even in Hollywood this is not so. Marriage is a serious relationship, taken seriously by the overwhelming majority of Americans today.

5. The fiction is that marriage solves personal problems. "If she's having difficulty, marriage will fix it up. All she needs is a good man." "All he needs is the steadying influence of a good woman," is the folklore. The actual fact coming out of a great deal of clinical evidence, as well as research studies, is that marriage very rarely solves personal problems. It brings its own problems, its own adjustments that require a great deal of maturity and further development. Marriage can no more be expected to straighten out a twisted personality than it can be expected to cure a crippled limb. We Americans expect far too much of marriage in terms of solving personal problems. Our young people need to recognize, far better than most of them do now, that their problems are not going to end at the altar. But rather that life, whether in marriage or outside, before or after

marriage, has its own developmental tasks, problems, crises, hazards that every individual must learn to face and to cope with as competently as possible. Marriage is a way of life, not a cure-all.

6. "There is no place for conflict in marriage. In a good Christian home there should be no differences, no raised voices, and no conflicts." This has been one of our most tenacious pieces of folklore. Actually, we have an overwhelming amount of evidence, clinical and statistical, that indicates without question that conflict is inevitable in any marriage. Marriages are based upon differences. Just the fact that men marry women brings together overwhelming differences in many unions. Women have been taught to respond to their various emotional states in everyday situations in quite different ways than men growing up as males have learned. Each person brings his own personality, his own temperament, his own way of looking at life, so that all through every moment of every day of every year in any marriage, from time to time, differences can be expected. The question is not, "Shall we flail out in open warfare, or swallow our differences and presume and pretend that they aren't there?" but rather, "How shall we learn to live with our differences as husband and wife, as person to person, as generation to generation, as children come?"

The big challenge to the Christian marriage is openly facing, frankly, honestly, lovingly, the differences that exist in this intimate on-going relationship, with the goal of learning to live together with those differences in such ways that bring joy and satisfaction and happiness rather than distress, frustration, and discontent.

7. "I'm not marrying her family, I'm marrying her," is the way you hear this fiction from the youngsters themselves. The belief is that marriage is a thing apart, and has very little to do with parents or the family relatives on either side. Studies today show conclusively that in-laws and relatives on both sides of the pair are very much a part of the marriage from the very beginning. Indeed, often they have had a hand in the courtship.

Many of these marriages would not have taken place if it had not been for the in-laws on both sides of the marriage helping out. This is true far more than most of our young people are willing to admit, or that most of us old enough to have marriageable youngsters widely recognize. The overwhelming fact today is that the average American couple today (as has always been the case) counts on a great deal of help from the older generation—financial help, emotional help, social help, and vocational help—as they get launched in their marriage. The marriage does not stand as a completely independent unit, but it is a part of the warp and woof of family life from the very beginning.

In-laws are a part of marriage, and when the first Christmas, the first baby, the first big bill comes along, the young couple find out that they married the family as well as each other. You will find much more about this in *In-Laws: Pro & Con,* and in some of the exciting reports from the Detroit Area study showing that in-laws and families are very much a part of the marriage from the very beginning.

8. Another fallacious piece of folklore that still persists in a great deal of the literature, that is heard among young people, and not so young people, is that if the sex life of the pair is good (if they follow the marriage manuals and do all the right things and have satisfied each other sexually) the marriage thereby is happy. Even that is not completely true. Dr. William Goode found even among the divorced pairs that he studied that many had good sex adjustment right up to the time of the divorce. Sex itself is not enough to hold a marriage together or to bring happiness to the pair.

Professor Judson Landis has found happy marriages even when there was very little sex satisfaction. He found couples happily married for twenty years or more where there had never been a really completely satisfying sex relationship.

It is interesting, particularly among religious groups, that we have tended to balloon up the importance of this biological act out of all proportion. This is not to say that sex does not belong in marriage. Quite the contrary, that is where it does belong. I'm not saying that most people do not find sexual satisfaction and fulfilment. That is not true. I am saying that sex in itself is not enough.

9. "It takes a baby to cement a marriage." "If they are having difficulties let them have a baby, and then the baby will hold the marriage together." Factually this is true only if these two people are really ready for parenthood. Only if they are mature enough to enjoy the privileges as well as the responsibilities of having a baby. Blood and Wolfe in the famous Detroit Area study, *Husbands and Wives,* found that, generally speaking, children are hard on marriage. They discovered that a marriage usually has its best years before the children come. Parenting in itself is difficult on the marriage relationship. Over the years while husband and wife are giving their prime attention to doing everything they can for the youngsters, the marriage itself tends to suffer.

Generally, communication between the spouses diminishes as the children come and grow up. The attention of the two parents tends to focus increasingly upon the children rather than upon each other. In the normal course of events the average marriage deteriorates as children continue to come and grow up. It's only after the last child has left home that the couple, with enough courage and innate love for each other, pick up the pieces of their own companionship and find the latter years the best that is yet to be.

In other words, we have been awfully sentimental about babies. They are precious, and I am not saying I do not love children. But I just refuse to wave the flag of motherhood and babydom blindly without recognizing the real responsibility, and the wear and tear on the adult relationship that a house full of children (or even one or two) normally is upon the marriage relationship.

10. We are told, to the place where we tell each other, that more marriages in America are breaking up now than ever before. The fact is that just is not so. Our divorce rate has

actually been decreasing since 1946 when we had a peak of divorces that came out of the poor war marriages consummated very hurriedly over a weekend leave. But ever since 1946 our divorce rate actually has been decreasing. "What's wrong with marriage" is all too frequent a theme of the fiction peddler who juggles estimates and twists figures in an effort to show that American marriage is instable and unhappy.

We have been told so constantly throughout recent years that American marriage is breaking up that we ourselves believe that one out of every three or four marriages has cracked up. Actually that is not and never has been true. Now, what is the situation? If we take the figures for any given year in the United States—so many marriage licenses and so many divorces—that would make a marriage/divorce ratio. But that does not count all the millions of us who were married in the beginning of the year, married at the end of the year, and kept on being happily married all through the year. You see the basic fallacy of this way of looking at the marriage/divorce ratio.

Now I am not saying that I am not concerned about divorces. I am giving my life to prevent divorce and to strengthen marriage so that we won't have these crack-ups. But I am saying that our panic about the increasing instability of American marriage has become an exaggeration that just is not borne out in research. For instance, the Joint Commission on Mental Health did a study of a representative sample of all men and women from all ways and walks of life, all age groups, all religions, all parts of the nation. When this was published in a number of volumes, one of which was called *Americans View Their Mental Health,* less than 5 per cent of all age groups of men and women were reported as saying that their marriages weren't too happy.

When Drs. Zimmerman and Cervantes studied thousands of married couples and their children, they found that 85 per cent of American families are essentially good families, in which husband and wife are finding satisfaction in each other and their relationship in marriage. They are sending their youngsters through school. They are keeping out of the headlines as troublemakers. They are keeping out of the hands of the police and keeping their children out of trouble.

It is time for us to face the facts and to begin to recognize what some of the tendencies and real trends are, both for good and as a challenge for the future.

One of the things that we are very frequently told, especially by our mass media, is that women today in the United States are unhappy. Married women are described as discontented, uninterested, "trapped," basically neurotic, and find no satisfaction in being women. Wives are said to find very little interest in their husbands or their children. This has been a fiction that has been often repeated and yet is basically fallacious, untrue, and unfortunate.

Robin Williams' study of married women out of Cornell University found that wives overwhelmingly "enjoy cooking interesting meals," say they don't hate housework, and list as their goals; (1) being a good wife—90 per cent of the married women in this study wanted first of all to be a good wife; (2) raising children properly—87 per cent; (3) being a religious person. Less than 25 per cent indicated their goals as women were "being creative and being successful on a job or other personally oriented interests." In other words, woman's primary concern today, as it has always been, centers in her husband, her children, and her family. And furthermore, she likes it that way.

Even woman's work is seen now by some of our most careful studies as essentially that of helping husband and children. When do wives work? During the early years of marriage when they are helping the husband raise the down payment on the house, buy the car or furnishings, and get the family established. Woman's ability and willingness to work is one of the reasons why she can get married in as large numbers and at an early age as she does. And, she does it by being available as a working partner.

The second most frequent time in a woman's life as a wife in which she can be expected to be a member of the labor force is when the children are headed for college and marriage. Characteristically, the American wife and mother today works during the early years of marriage to get the husband and the home established. Then she goes back into the labor force about the time the oldest has reached high school. Why? To get enough reserve so she and her husband can give their children the advantages that both of them have dreamed the children would have—getting them through college, getting them married, and getting them established generally.

Dr. Lois Hayden Meek Stolz, who many of you will recognize as one of our prime researchers in human development, recently published a review of more than fifty studies on the effects of the working mother on her children, on her marriage, on her home, and on herself as a personality. She could find no significant difference in any of these studies that came directly out of the woman's working itself. She found neglectful mothers, poor mothers, unhappy mothers among the unemployed as well as the employed women. Her conclusions were that the fact of the woman's working in itself didn't seem to make any difference. When the woman had skills to sell, when she had a co-operative husband, when her children were well cared for, when she could replace herself in the home without strain, when she found fulfilment in the work, when her marriage was provided for around the edges of her work responsibility, there was no particularly deleterious effect on her children, her husband, or on herself. You can find this research study in *Child Development*, December, 1960—sixty of the best pages of goblin-chasing that I have read on working mothers.

The Detroit Area study asked women what they expected of marriage, what satisfactions their marriage brought them, what they wanted most from their marriage. Now these are women in a large industrial area. They are not in comfortable little suburbs and towns. They are pretty much under the pressure of their communities, and yet these women said that they valued marriage, in rank order, for: (1) companionship; (2) a chance to have children; (3) the understanding and emotional support that they get from this intimate relation; (4) love and affection; (5) financial benefit (a poor fifth percentagewise). In other words, the picture of women as gold diggers, grabbing, neurotic, unhappy, discontented, irresponsible creatures is utterly untrue. American wives and mothers today, as they always have, are finding basic satisfaction in the central roles within the family.

Well, now what about men? It seems to me that men, too, have been terribly downgraded. The picture of the average American father on television is a combination between Casper Milquetoast and a laughable kind of creature who always gets the thin end of the deal from his wife, his youngsters, his neighbors, and everyone else.

Husbands have been considered in popular literature as being henpecked individuals who live in a matriarchy, leave their homes in the morning, drudge through the day in their offices, come back only to pick up the crumbs of affection, attention, companionship for which they are earning their sustenance. This is not so either.

Representative studies across the country tell us that domination by women in America has been greatly exaggerated. Men in general still control their families, and whatever henpecked husbands do exist are not victims of shrewish wives but of their own inadequacy. They are henpecked because they are incompetent. They do less around the home than men of influence. The more prestige a man has at work, the more money he makes, the higher his status, the more decisions he makes at home. In other words, the man of competence is as great an influence in his home as he is in the business world outside.

Dr. Kenkel and others have found that women *want* their husbands to have greater authority. They want to look to their husbands as the chief element of control and authority in the family. They look to their husbands for opinions and want them to make the basic decisions. Women want to have a voice, but they want to look up to their husbands. In the experience that I have had as a marriage counselor through the years, as well as in my own family, this has been borne out almost all of the time.

Most of us as women want a man we can look up to, respect, and lean on as the tower of strength, authority, and control within the home. Husbands and wives today are closer now that they both share more of the same education and find each other through the selective courtship processes that we talked about earlier. Fathers today seem to enjoy their children more, since they are closer to them than traditionally was true. Now that fathers are participating in child care and child guidance and hearing their children's discussions and problems, they are closer to them.

Men have more interest in the family than traditionally was true. This is particularly the case in so many of our homes that are electrically and electronically controlled. There is more to interest a man and more things for which a man is needed in the family than formerly was the case.

There seems to be conclusive evidence that men today understand women and children better than their own grandfathers did. They are more sensitive, more tender, and more satisfied with the relationship within marriage and family.

The time has come to recognize that there is little place for fallacious folklore about marriage amid the powerful realities of today's homes. We do have a great many unsolved problems that are tremendous challenges and should concern any who are working in the field of marriage and family or with youth preparing for marriage and family.

The time has come to slay the witches of doom, to get the goblins of exaggeration that still appear in press, screen, pulpit, and coffee klatch. It is time to come to know the truth about marriage as it really is today with all of its challenges and its promises. There is power in the heart of the family that may one day equal the power at the core of the atom—as soon as we can show parallel discipline in studying and releasing it. That is our challenge.

2
Being Married

We Americans are the most married people on earth. More of us get married, at least once, than is true for any other people around the globe. We are getting married in larger numbers and in greater proportion than used to be true even here in our own country. At the turn of the century only about two-thirds of our women ever got married. The others were the unclaimed treasures who taught Sunday school and helped bring up their married sister's children. Today, the great majority of our girls and our boys not only get married, but they get married at younger ages, and they anticipate getting married for years before the actual event.

Studies of high school and college students across the country in recent years, such as the 1960 study published under the title *What College Students Think,* found, to no one's real surprise, that one of the central goals of today's students on the campuses across the country is for the kind of marriage and family life where they can find fulfilment individually and through families. From the girl's point of view, a good marriage assures her of emotional support and basic security—a home of her own, husband, children, and fulfilment as a woman.

Equally as many young men today in our high schools and colleges indicate, in these national polls, that marriage and family are central in their dreams too.

A successful marriage for a man provides a solid basis for his

12

vocational, social, emotional, physical, and spiritual life through the years. He and his girl expect a great deal of marriage, and they begin to dream of it many years before they meet at the altar.

Our young people today are relatively free to marry when they will, and large numbers are getting married at younger ages than ever before. They are getting married before the girl has finished her educational plans, and oftentimes before the fellow has finished his. They are getting married frequently before the man has established himself in his vocation or even completed his responsibilities for military service. They are getting married at young ages with a freedom and with an opportunity that has been unheard of in preceding generations.

At the turn of the century a man typically was in his twenty-seventh year before he had earned enough to be ready to support a wife and family. He was in his twenty-seventh year before he asked Grandma's parents for her hand. Young Joe today, his great grandson, is barely twenty-two when he gets up the nerve to ask the girl *herself* to get married. She is usually willing to keep her job so that she and her husband can finance a house, a car, a baby, and all of the rest.

These young people of ours are free, not only to marry when they will, but in a rather new way they are free to marry whom they will. With this unique freedom of choice comes a very real responsibility. Always before in our culture, as, indeed, is true in most of the cultures around the world, the families of the young people took the prime responsibility for seeing that their sons and daughters were teamed up appropriately with the kinds of mates who would be good for them to live with.

Nowadays our young people grow up together in large, coeducational elementary, junior high, and senior high schools, and they go on to coeducational colleges and universities. They have the freedom and the very real responsibility of choosing, out of the available eligibles who will have them, the one individual whom they dream of living with the rest of their lives. These are serious dreams.

Our young people count upon marriage lasting a lifetime. The vast majority of them, in poll after poll, are found to take marriage very seriously. You sometimes hear that today's young people have their fingers crossed as it were, expecting that if it doesn't work out they can get a divorce. This kind of attitude just is not so. In poll after poll we find that the vast majority of our young people look upon marriage as a very serious, permanent relationship in which they expect to find the kind of happiness, the kind of satisfaction, the kind of mutual responsibility that we hope they will find.

Unfortunately, as you know, too many of these marriages flounder. Particularly the very young marriages find the going difficult. However, within recent decades we have begun to understand some of the very real reasons why some marriages succeed and others fail, so that now, with some relative assurance, we can almost outline the main ingredients of a good marriage.

Think of what a woman's magazine looks like these days with all the recipes for good things to eat and the ways of fixing up the house attractively. But when you get to the section on marriage, child-rearing, and people living together in families, the pages usually are given, not to what makes for success, but rather to the problems and the troubles and all of the mistakes that people have made. If we did the same thing in the pages that have to do with recipes, we would have articles on "How I failed with my first souffle," "How I made a mess of our living room," or "I'll never go to that furniture store again." Yet this has been our attitude about marriage as expressed in popular writing.

Some of us have begun to realize that we can take almost as intelligent, constructive, and creative an attitude toward marriage as we do toward these other areas of life. Let us review in very quick outline some of the factors that make for success in marriage—that have turned up time and time again in many hundreds of pieces of research with many hundreds of thousands of couples over the last thirty or more years.

Good people make good marriages.—A marriage is no better than the human material that goes into it. We find documentation upon documentation at this point. We know from a considerable amount of statistical research, as well as a great deal of clinical evidence, that wholesome, well-adjusted persons provide a solid base for the kind of companionship that both husband and wife tend to look for in marriage as the central value. Contrariwise, the individual who has never gotten along very well with anybody, who couldn't get along with a roommate in college, who is always having difficulties in his human relationships, very likely is not a much more comfortable person to live with in the family. The individual who learned early and since has been refining his skills of getting along, not only comfortably and smoothly, but also creatively with others, is good marriage material. He is able to take his skills into his relationships with wife and children and find the companionship and the creative adjustments that any relationship involves.

One piece of research coming out of Northwestern University found that the marriages with a minimum of neurotic traits in both partners make the best go of it. The individual who is touchy, moody, and hard to get along with, generally speaking, is touchy, moody, and hard to get along with in marriage. Marriage is a series of situations in which individuals either practice the relative wholesomeness or the relative neuroticism of their personalities.

Good marriages are made by the husbands and wives who have learned to be loving persons.—These are people who have *learned* the art of loving, as Erich Fromm so beautifully puts it. They have learned in their own growing up as personalities how to really care for others in the double sense. It is that wonderful empathy that some people have so warmly you can feel it in a handshake. This kind of sensitivity, this kind of awareness, this kind of warm outgoingness blesses any human contact, either in the family or out. It characterizes the warm, nurturing, loving person who gets most from marriage, gives most to marriage, and brings up warm, loving, outgoing children.

Drs. Burgess, Cottrell, and Wallin, and others have been publishing reports of longitudinal marriage research through the years since the 1930's. They first selected a group of a thousand engaged couples, followed them on into marriage, and now have begun to publish how those couples are faring as middle-aged couples, twenty and twenty-five years later. One of the very first things found in these longitudinal studies was that happiness runs in families. Happiness of the parents' marriage is significantly related to the children's happiness. This in turn is related significantly to the happiness of the families that those children make.

It is almost as though those individuals who have learned the ways of living together lovingly, successfully, happily, communicate these successful ways of family living quite as really as we parents communicate the language of speech that our children learn from our lips. Living in a happy home, almost without realizing it, they pick up those skills, those habits, those attitudes, those ways of living together that in turn make them the kind of people who have what it takes to make a happy marriage.

When I am making this point with young people, as I very frequently do, I always feel impelled to rush in here with a great big parenthesis. Otherwise, many of our young people quite rightly will shrug their shoulders and say, "There is no chance for me . . . my folks are divorced, or they are living in a kind of cold war, for nothing my mom can do will satisfy dad and the other way around." The antidote for this fatalistic attitude is *the determination to succeed.* Success can be worked for out of a given combination of inherited and environmental conditions. The youngster, for instance, who has grown up in an unhappy home can, during the second decade of life when human beings are beginning to emancipate themselves from their families, look back at his parental home and say, "Now, believe me, when I get married I am going to do things differently." This two-way look at marriage gives young people a chance to evaluate their past in terms of their future. This is one reason why these are good years for education in family living.

I had a very interesting situation in one of the college classes I was teaching some years ago that illustrates this point. I had just concluded the very first meeting of a college class that would continue on through the term. It was a fairly large one, and I had not yet gotten acquainted with all of the students. As they all left the room, one of the fellows who had apparently been seated way at the back came up and said, "Dr. Duvall, I want you to know why I am taking this course." I smiled acceptingly and he continued. "You see, Susie and I are engaged to be married. We realize we have two strikes against us, because Susie's folks were divorced when she was still in junior high school, and she has grown up six months in one home and six months in the other. My folks aren't divorced. They are still living together but in that kind of armed truce in which everything my mother does rubs my father the wrong way.

"I don't want Susie to do that to me. I don't want to do to Susie what I have seen my father do to my mother through the years, until she is her very worst self when she is with him. Susie and I want to learn what it takes to start fresh, to build strong the kind of relationship in the kind of marriage that we want our home to be." It's this determination to succeed that is quite as strong as some of these other factors out of the environment of the parents' marriage.

Boys and girls who grow up in churches, who have spiritual roots, who remain active in a religious fellowship of whatever denomination, who have a service orientation, are individuals who make significantly happier and more permanent marriages than those with no religious roots, or who have broken with the church, or today find little significance in a life of service. Statistical studies find a disproportionately large number of successful marriages among ministers, teachers, social workers, and others who live lives of service. Those who fall at the bottom of the list with more failures, more divorces, more annulments, and more difficulty and heartache are significantly those whose orientation in their occupation is toward using rather than serving persons. There have been a lot of jokes about the traveling salesman, and so I always hate to mention him as bottom of the heap. But he is, and I am sure the only reason isn't the farmer's daughter. Rather, we need to recognize that the salesman has been taught to see the other person as a market to be exploited.

There has been a great deal of recognition that the Hollywood marriage is less stable than some of the less conspicuous marriages, without realizing, perhaps, that the Hollywood personality sees other persons as audiences and expects admiration and adulation of them. Such a stance toward others makes for uncomfortable marriages. Good families are those in which the members love and serve each other in mutual devotion.

Good marriages are made by persons who are trustworthy, responsible individuals with a great deal of mutual respect for one another.—This point first came out almost fifteen years ago when Harvey Locke did a study, comparing divorced couples with happily married couples, in an effort to find out what the difference is between those who break up and those who continue living together happily. He found the one factor of *responsibility* looming very large as a conspicuously significant difference between the two samples. Those whose marriage had broken were made up far more frequently of irresponsible husbands and wives who did not carry their own responsibilities for their roles in marriage. Whereas, the happily married couples were made up of persons who were responsible, who carried their end of the load, who did what was expected, who could be trusted, and who had mutual respect for their spouses, both as men and women.

I usually remind young people at this point that, after all, being married means sharing a great deal of everything you have and are. It means sharing the keys to your car. It means sharing all of the accommodations and resources of the family. It means sharing your most agonizing disappointments, your most wonderful successes and dreams. So, if you can't basically trust each other, your marriage is on shaky ground.

Good marriages are made by good people who have what it

takes to build one of the most intimate, one of the most demanding, one of the most permanent relationships in our entire culture. A man does not expect to stay on the same job all his life. He expects to move on to bigger and better things as he gets going vocationally. There is no mark of shame at all if a man has quit his job and found another. How differently we look upon marriage! We expect to be married permanently and thereby demand a great deal of ourselves and each other. Good marriages are made by good people.

Good marriages are made by congenial couples who share a similar life style.—More than 167 different pieces of research to date find that there is a tendency for persons to marry individuals like themselves. We tend to marry persons of the same general socioeconomic background, from the same religious faith, within the same cultural group. We tend to marry individuals who are basically like ourselves. As one boy very delightfully put it, "When the time came and I was ready to marry, I looked around and found a girl who was dreaming my dreams and thinking my thoughts and finishing my sentences, and so I took her hand and got married." It was almost as simple or as complex as that.

There is a great deal of concern and interest about the mixed marriage today. There is every reason to believe that the mixed marriage is here to stay in our American culture. Indeed, Dr. John Thomas, author of *The American Catholic Family,* expresses his concern as a Roman Catholic that the mixed marriages of members of his faith with non-Catholics are very definitely on the increase, for good and sufficient reasons coming out of our kind of culture. It is probably time to recognize that some mixed marriages can work and do, and make exceedingly sound, courageous, valuable, happy homes. But, all of the research that has been thus far completed indicates that a mixed marriage is often a difficult marriage to build, requiring more work, a great deal more maturity, and a considerably longer period of time until the two people are one.

Sometimes when I am making this point with young people, I

put it this way. If you grow up in the same church, pretty much the same kind of family, in the same kind of community, then you talk the same language, you get through to each other across a very short gulf relatively easily, because things have the same meaning for you and you both feel the same way. You have been brought up the same way. But, if he grows up in one church and she another, if he grows up in one kind of family and she another, if they both come from entirely different cultural groups, then there is a wide social gulf between them that must somehow be bridged—the kind of bridge of communication across which each can get through to the other with understanding in all of the many day-by-day situations that marriage inevitably brings. Therefore, the mixed marriage must be worked on, must be built diligently over a long period of time.

More of our mixed marriages break up in divorce, separation, and annulment than is true of marriages within the same religious faith, within the same social group. You will find upon closer inspection that in a very real way every marriage is a mixed marriage. Just the fact that men marry women makes it a mixed marriage. We need to recognize that women are taught to respond to frustration, disappointment, elation, joy, and sorrow in a woman's way, whereas men growing up in the same society, and yet never quite the same culture, learn a man's way of responding to exasperation, frustration, joy, sorrow, disappointment, and elation.

Studies at Northwestern University indicate that we tend in our mate selection to choose mates who complement our personalities. For instance, the slow, steady man is quite apt to marry the kind of effervescent, outgoing girl who flutters about him. He becomes her Rock of Gibraltar and she's the sparkle in his ginger ale, and they both love it until one gets exasperated at the other.

A number of years ago I was on a married couple's forum in a Jewish Temple, of which Dr. Joshua Liebman, whose *Peace of Mind* you may have read, was the rabbi. On that panel with Dr.

Liebman and myself there was a young psychiatrist from the Harvard School of Medicine. Instead of making a speech that night, as the rest of us dutifully did because we were expected to, the creative young psychiatrist passed out index cards all across the auditorium. He saw to it that everybody had a pencil. Then he said, "Now on the first side of this index card I want each of you, as quickly as possible, to write down the very first thing that attracted you to the person you married." Everybody grinned patiently and did what the doctor asked. And then he said, "All right, turn your cards over now and, as quickly as you can, write the very first thing that pops into your mind that annoys and irritates you about this same individual." They dutifully started writing, and suddenly there was a wave of laughter over the entire assemblage of married couples. He said, "That's my talk. The very thing that attracted you to each other in the first place is usually the thing that most frequently irritates you in each other. Because you are not carbon copies of one another, and did not want to be in the first place."

I shall never forget a conference I participated in years ago with some of my professional colleagues in which there was a very delightful and perceptive anthropologist from France. We had a week-long discussion of the differences between men and women. Experts' papers were making a big deal of how different the two sexes are. By the end of the week one was almost sure that man and woman could not possibly live together; they were just too different. Then, this very delightful French anthropologist stood up in the back of the lecture hall. He was so small he had to stand on a chair, and he took his hanky out of his breast pocket, and he waved it and said, "Vive la différence."

Every marriage is a mixed marriage. All of us must learn to live with difference and to enjoy our differences. As we learn these basic lessons within our families, we have, very possibly, the very seeds of the kind of just and lasting peace we are dreaming of for the world around us.

It takes mature, prepared persons to make a go of marriage these days. The individual must be mature enough, old enough, and ready to settle down—ready to take on not only the responsibilities but the privileges that marriage provides. These things are related to genuine maturity. The United States Bureau of the Census and many, many studies all point in the same direction—that, statistically speaking, the teen-age marriage tends to be risky. Too few of our teen-agers have grown up enough to be ready for the demands, the realities, the complexities of marriage today.

The happily married couple more often has taken long enough to get acquainted, has had a long enough courtship and an adequate engagement to bring them to the place where they are really ready to join together as man and wife. They have developed the kind of empathy, sensitivity to each other's feelings, a sense of unity, an ability to love and to be loved. That couple who have given the test of time to their relationship far more frequently go on through the years together than is true of the whirlwind courtship. The couple succeed who have given their relationship the opportunity for the slow, deep, meaningful growth that a relationship, as well as an individual, apparently needs. Maturity then of the relationship, as well as of the individual, is what good marriages are made of.

Preparation for marriage includes understanding of the roles that are expected as husband and wife, father and mother. This means, of course, adequate sex education. It means an awareness of what goes on in marriage, of the wonder and the miracle of the story of creation that has been shared with us mere humans by the Father of us all. It includes the skills of communication—the ability to get through to each other in all the many ways in which human beings yearn to associate.

Dr. O. Spurgeon English observes that it is not enough just to love each other; you must love marriage as man loves truth or beauty or justice. The people who make a go of marriage have the attitude of loving marriage with all of its challenge and all of its possibilities.

Being married is fairly simple today. Even children, before they are at all ready to found a home, can find each other and get married. But staying happily married through the years is a real challenge today, amidst the hazards of changing roles of men and women, of great expectations of each other and of marriage itself, and the threats of a great deal of confusion, fallacious folklore, superstition, and taboo that have little place in a scientific culture like ours.

But there are rewards, too, to match these hazards: rewards of building an island of peace in the midst of the troubled seas of the twentieth century; the promise of developing together an emotional climate that will be good to grow in through the years, that will bless not only those within the home but all those who have contact with it; satisfactions of growing and sinking roots deep into the spiritual soil in which they and their children may grow.

Being married today presents the challenge of creating a citadel of strength amidst the stresses and strains of the explosive world situation. Having hold of that great power of love that is nurtured within the family may, if we are wise enough and have enough disciplined attention, one day match that great power that has so recently been released at the heart of the atom.

3

Friendship Finding
and
Mate Selection

Young people are free to choose their mates as never before has been possible for them. Indeed, today young people are responsible for finding their own friends and choosing their own mates. In an earlier day, and in most of the other cultures of the world, as well as our own, there was a great deal of assistance from members of the family.

My husband and I were in Bangalore some years ago and led a group of one hundred young college women in a most interesting discussion in which the girls were divided right down the middle. Fifty said that they wanted a modern "love marriage," and the other 50 per cent quite articulately indicated that they preferred an arranged marriage. As one very attractive young woman put it, "My daddy will know who is best for me to have as a husband." This young woman had grown up in a world in which her contacts with young men were very limited, and she quite rightly recognized that when the time came her father would find the kind of man who would make her a good husband. Our young people are coming along in freer situations where the opportunity and the responsibility of finding one's mate is on the young people themselves.

In an earlier day here in America there was still a great deal of influence on the part of families. In the county in which I grew up I can well remember that our families arranged all sorts of social occasions in which those of us who were potentially congenial might meet and engage in a variety of activities that would possibly be, not only of interest in themselves, but bring us to an interest in each other. The traditional assistance that the older generation always has given young people is today at a minimum.

Now when our young people at very early ages attend large consolidated schools they are thrown with many different types of young people from as many types of backgrounds. They represent various religious faiths with different ideas and ideals, dreams and aspirations. They move in a kind of heterogeneity from which they have to choose those persons who will serve them best as friends. This is a great deal to ask of young teen-agers.

One of the things that teen-agers have themselves invented to take care of this very complex responsibility is the practice of going steady. A young pair who are sure of each other will date each other exclusively, cling to each other, often to the dismay of the elders. What it means to young people is not just what it seems to mean from our point of view as adults. As one very attractive sophomore girl put it in my hearing not very long ago, "Sure, I go steady with Harry. I know I can manage anything he thinks up in an evening and I wouldn't be quite so sure with some of the other possible dates I could get."

In spite of the fact that our young people from the very early teens are thrown into contact with a great many other young people of their own age and of both sexes, the vast majority of these youngsters say that they are lonely and want more friends, and that they need help in finding and selecting friends. A recent Purdue Opinion Panel found that 66 per cent of the boys and 70 per cent of the girls said that they wanted more friends. When one of our great religious groups here in this country studied teen-agers in their denomination in 1959, they found that the three outstanding concerns of the young people were: friends, family, and the future.

Another factor that needs to be put into context is the high mobility of American families, by which statistically one out of every five families moves from one home to another in any given year. This is particularly true of families with children. Once a family gets fairly well settled, it tends to stay put for a longer period of time. While there are children the family tends to move far more frequently than it does in the later stages of family life cycle. Moving is hard on teen-agers. It's difficult for youngsters to pull up roots, to say good-by to persons of both sexes who have come to mean a great deal, particularly in the second decade of life. These relationships with peers tend to be terribly important, because they are the very first experience that a youngster has in finding himself as a member of his generation in new, unique, and personal ways.

Therefore, it becomes increasingly important that we who work with youth know and help youth to understand what the principles of friendship finding tend to be. Fortunately for our youngsters, as well as for ourselves, there has been a great deal of research on this matter over the period of the last twenty years. The research started during World War II when the Air Force and the Army and the Navy needed to know a great deal about small groups. They studied about which men would get along well enough with what other fellows so that they could be trusted over long periods of time in a submarine, in a lonely army camp, or a bomber. Unfortunately, a lot of this very exciting research that has other applications is buried in academic and military files, until an occasional person gets interested and digs it out.

Research into who gets along with whom, who makes friends with whom, who can be predicted to click with whom started then with the military, where most of our money still flows. Then it was picked up immediately after the war by our housing project people, particularly those who were concerned with the large public housing project and who recognized that the morale in a housing project was largely dependent upon the feeling that the families got as members of the group, as members of the neighborhood, as members of the project sharing similar accommodations. The housing project people found the same general principles that the military had found. Some of our summer camp people got interested about that time and began making similar experiments in summer camps, and they came out with the same answers. In other words, there are principles that work among human beings whether they are in the military, in housing projects, or in summer camps—wherever they meet they tend to pull together certain kinds of people in predictable ways.

1. First of all is the principle of *accessibility*. We tend to find our friends from among those with whom we have continuing close contact. The research that has been going on in housing projects finds that it's the families who not only live closest together who get closest to each other in friendship formation; indeed, it's those who share the same hallways, who get their mail from the same general lobbies, who use the same stairways, whose garbage collection comes from the same general area, who meet each other in these homely, everyday situations day after day in continuing contact. They are the ones who invite each other in for meals, who run in and out of each other's homes for cups of coffee, baby sitting, and all of the rest.

They found that it was the fellows in the boys' camps who lived near the dining room or who were on the way to the lavatories, or who slept in the lower bunks near the door who ended up at the end of the summer with more friends than the fellows on the top bunks, way off away from the dining room, or in the back of the huts. Now this has a lot to say if you begin to think about it in terms of the way we make arrangements for some of these youngsters that need a boost. Don't tuck them in a corner on a top bunk is one of the implications. Get them where they will have continued ongoing contact with others.

One of the other aspects of this accessibility principle is put in terms of a little formula that I have used with young people when I tell them that it is the girl who can do things that goes places. As a young person develops a great many skills and abilities and interests, these interests of his or hers take that youngster out into areas and situations where other young people with similar interests are. For instance, the girl who sings in the choir goes, not only to choir on Sunday mornings and Sunday evenings, but to choir practice. She gets to walk home with the others, boys or girls, and both are important. She gets interested in musical things, goes to concerts, and begins, perhaps, to be interested in a musical instrument. Her music takes her out into the musical world where other musically interested persons are.

The girl who gets interested in drama, the boy who gets involved in sports, finds himself (or herself) increasingly accessible to other individuals who share similar interests. This is one of the significant differences between the young person who has a great many friends, feels that he belongs and is accepted, and develops thereby the kind of self-confidence that is so important in the second decade of life, and the young person who is lonely and discouraged and feels so much out of his own generation that he oftentimes becomes a dropout, even though intellectually and academically he has what it takes to continue growing. These are terribly important things. We as adults have tended to take all too lightly the importance of friendships during the teen years. They are critical in terms of the future of the young person.

2. There is another principle that is very closely related to accessibility and yet different enough to bear looking at separately. That is the factor of *congeniality* or similarity. We have already alluded to this in part by saying that the musical person tends to associate with and make friends with the musical person, and so with the religiously oriented person, the academically-minded, the intellectual, and so forth.

The Coleman studies, *The Adolescent Society,* of ten Midwest high schools over a period of several years found with almost frightening clarity that, regardless of whether the high school was a technical school in a big industrial area or in a well-to-do suburban community preparing young people for college, the American high school today is made up of a number of subcultures. Very few of our students have access across these cultural groups, or cliques as the kids call them, within the adolescent society. Generally speaking, it's the athletes and the sports crowd among the boys who are the "big wheels," leading the parade in the social life of the high school. It is the socially active girls, the junior equivalent to the country club set, who tend to be the most popular and get elected to the various positions by their schoolmates.

The youngsters who belong to the religious crowd and dutifully go to church and relate themselves to religious activities as your youngsters and mine do are very rarely even close to the top of the heap. And "the brains" in many of these schools—those with a probable future to contribute to the world—actually feel like squares, or, as the kids put it, "cubes," because they have such a very marginal position in the social life of the community.

These are actually counterparts of the larger community, in which most individuals find their social lives within a relatively small proportion of any community. Every community is made up of little social worlds in which central core interests are shared, and very few of us actually make friends with a large number of persons from many, many social worlds.

These two factors—accessibility and congeniality—are so important (even though they sound very simple, as though we have always known them) that social scientists, with them in mind, went into one of our large coeducational universities and were able to predict in late September who would be friends with whom in the Freshman class by Christmas time. And, they hit it on the head. In other words, here is an ability to predict. If you keep in focus accessibility and congeniality you actually can predict human behavior in terms of friendship-finding.

When we get this kind of knowledge working for us in our work with young people we will begin to be not only scientific in our ability to predict, but also we will become increasingly effective in what we are doing with and for our young people.

Social skills go beyond the ability to handle a tennis racket or put on a pair of skates. They go beyond these activities and encompass a great many of the skills that have to do with how you relate yourself to other human beings.

In the Havighurst *et al.* longitudinal research, *Growing Up in River City*, a team of research workers went into a city on the Mississippi River and studied all of the young people in the public schools who were in the sixth grade eight years ago. Then intensively over the years they followed those youngsters up out of junior high school through senior high school and on into what followed senior high. They found that social adjustment (ability to get along comfortably with members of one's own generation and with teachers and other adults) was significantly related, not only to the general social life of the young person, but to the sense of identity that young person was establishing. The kind of person that he had a feeling he was becoming, the kind of thing that oftentimes makes the difference in what he does and what he does not do in a given situation because of what he feels he is, his confidence in himself, is a sense of his growing identity.

Interestingly enough, social adjustment was one of the three critical factors that had to do with the predictability of whether that young person would go on through school, develop his talents, and work near the top of his ability. IQ was not as important as social adjustment as a predictive factor. The three factors in order of importance were: (1) social adjustment, (2) family background (the kind of family he came from, what his dad did, whether they had books in the family, his mother's educational level, and so forth), and (3) IQ.

The University of Michigan Survey Research Center has conducted two nation-wide studies of adolescence. One of the questions asked was, "Who is the girl that everybody likes?" Of the girls, 84 per cent said, "The girl that everybody likes is aware of everyone." Almost two thirds, 63 per cent, said, "She is nice to everyone." In other words, the popular girl is an outgoing, sensitive, aware person who is nice to everyone. Interestingly enough, only 17 per cent of these girls said the girl whom everybody likes is good looking, attractive, nicely dressed, well groomed. When you reflect on the preoccupation that our adolescent girls put in on hair, face, clothes, and grooming and find that only 17 per cent think that is really important in terms of the girl everybody likes, you begin to realize how distorted our adolescent practices are in terms of their own beliefs.

Adolescent boys were asked the same question: "Who is the boy whom everyone likes?" And 72 per cent of them said practically the same thing, "He's a friendly guy." Another 30 per cent said, "He is nice to everyone." One fourth, 25 per cent, said, "He is good looking"—even more than the adolescent girls in responding to the same question. And, interestingly enough, only 15 per cent said, "He is good in sports." In other words, it looks as if boys follow the big wheels in sports, but they do not necessarily like them. This is something that our youngsters, particularly in our church and religious settings, need to understand—that being popular and being elected captain of the football team is not necessarily the kind of thing that makes one a person who has friends and who is generally liked.

The River City studies found also that the young people who are growing up in the churches of a community tend to develop leadership that is not apparent in the large public schools. In other words, one of the things we are doing in our church youth programs is developing an inherent leadership that would not have arisen in our large public high schools, geared as they are to giving leadership positions to the sports crowd among the boys and the very socially prominent girls who do not always go to our churches.

Young people today, growing up in the midst of complex, complicated social situations where social adjustment is recognized as so centrally important for their developing into human beings, need *graduated opportunities* for developing social skills with young people of their own kind, as well as others, in wholesome, encouraging settings. This means that the church youth program is truly important. It is something that our young people need. They need graduated opportunities so that they may, one by one, develop the skills that lead to more complicated and advanced levels of social interaction. For instance, young people during junior high school age should not be expected (regardless of their religious connections and what their denomination says) to be adequate in a social dance situation. Why? Not just because the church says, "No," but because it goes against the grain of human development.

The junior high school youngster is grappling with problems of how to carry on a conversation, how to get himself into a group, how to greet another individual, how to accept an invitation, how to refuse an invitation, how to do all sorts of complicated things in which he needs experience in simple, less demanding, less complicated activities. When we arrange for our junior high school youngsters to have a picnic or a skating party or some of the singing games (where it is a touch and go kind of thing, where you touch and look and then go on without having to do anything about it yet), you are planning the kind of activity that is geared to that youngster's development.

In a new piece of research in which we explored all of the students in junior and senior high schools in representative communities across the country, we asked them the question about going steady. We found that going steady is practically universal in some communities, but that in communities such as are found in Utah, going steady is practically nonexistent, especially in the junior high school. There it is not until the students get way along in senior high school that there is any going steady to speak of at all. Why? Possibly because Mormons have for years emphasized wholesome recreation for young people in groups, and they have enough dedicated adults to get these youngsters out in the summer for picnics, barbecues, and trips. They take them everywhere in groups. They sing on their way to the place, and they sing on their way back, and they have a perfectly wonderful time without pairing off and leaving the kids all alone with nothing to do but explore each other. The churches, the communities, that make provision for graduated social opportunities for youngsters do not have the problems of going steady and what goes with too-early going steady.

There are probably other cultural groups (very possibly you are helping create them for your young people in many situations) , where you do not have all of these early marriages—"the have-to," "the bang-bang marriages," as the kids put them. You do not have these problems because you have not allowed the circumstances that bring them into being. You have prepared for graduated opportunities for young people to learn how to relate themselves wholesomely to each other, step by step, until they come to the threshold of marriage. Then they understand themselves; they understand each other; they understand the social situations and can conduct themselves, not only sensibly, but maturely and responsibly in line with their central orientations.

Thirty or more years ago we would have young people list on the blackboard all of the qualities they were going to look for in a mate. Then the problem was matching up anybody who would come up to all these qualities. He must be honest, he must be religious, he must be loving, he must have a sense of humor, and all the rest. It actually had about as little to do with reality as one could imagine. Today we are recognizing you do not choose a mate the way you pick out an automobile. When you select a car you can look over a number of models, you can try them out, you can ask the man who owns one. When you choose a car you pick one model out of several that are currently available. When you choose a mate, all the choice you get is to take it or leave it. Is this particular friendship something that I want to continue or break off? One of the most frequent questions I get from both girls and boys is, "How do you get rid of good old Joe?" The boys put it, "How do I get my girl back in circulation? She has given me the best weeks of her life."

You do not select a mate out of all of the millions of eligibles of the other sex of your age and general background. But rather you must have three things: (1) You must have a sufficient number of acquaintances to insure a range of individuals from which a choice can be made. (2) You must achieve sufficient depth in your acquaintances to be able to appraise their marriageability. In other words, you must get well enough acquainted to ask yourself, "Is he really somebody I would be seriously interested in?" "Is she really my kind of girl?" Mutual compatibility then and a possible marriageability come out of sufficient depth of acquaintance over a period of time. (3) You must be able to involve others and to make possible commitments yourself if you are to reach the stage of making a firm choice. You will find these three spelled out in detail in the new *Being Married,* in which we have brought all of these research pieces into focus for young people themselves.

1. We know that mates are chosen overwhelmingly on the principle of *homogamy*. We tend to marry persons like ourselves and that there are reasons for this. One of the reasons why we tend to marry persons like ourselves is that we tend to find our friends from those like ourselves. In other words, homogamy grows out of homophily *(homo-philia)*. We choose our friends on the basis of similarity, and we find our mates from among our friends. It is as simple as that.

2. A second factor that is very important is that we psychologically tend to choose our mates resembling individuals with whom we have had significantly meaningful relationships. Research studies find that unconsciously we tend to try to continue relationships that have been satisfying. "I Want a Girl—Just Like the Girl That Married Dear Old Dad" is the old song. And, there's something to it psychologically. If the girl that married good old Dad has been a satisfying kind of woman that a boy has loved and has not had to fight off through the years, who has allowed him to develop, then that boy is deeply satisfied in his relationship with his mother and tends to marry the kind of girl who in many ways subconsciously reminds him of her. This is a very important principle.

Mate selection is usually on the basis of either reproduction or repudiation of the role patterns that mother and father have played in the home. Our youngsters either reproduce what they like or they repudiate what they do not like. Therefore, you tend to find mates who very much resemble or are as opposite as possibly could be. This is one of the ways to explain the ones who kick over the traces and go off and marry some "impossible" kind of mate.

3. Third is the social pressure of friends and family. If a youngster begins to be seriously interested in somebody from his own church, his own way of life, who comes from a family like the one he comes from, his parents and her parents approve. They bless the relationship. They make it possible for the youngsters to see more and more of each other. Their approval greases the skids for the courtship process that leads to marriage. Friends similarly back, support, and encourage a suitable combination. But let a youngster from one church fall in love with or begin to get involved with a youngster from another entirely different faith, or another background, and you find friends and families on both sides of the situation tending to oppose, to disapprove, and to set up blocks to the relationship.

These three factors tend to support homogamy. But there are reasons, too, why the mixed marriage is on the increase—and is here to stay. One of the big reasons for mixed marriage is the increasing mobility of our population in which communication between various ethnic, cultural, religious, socioeconomic groups is bringing our melting pot to a boil.

Young people today grow up with far more tolerant attitudes, as seen in the research, for instance, on, "Would you marry a person of another faith?" There is far more tolerance, far more acceptance of difference, than just a generation or so ago.

Secondly, mixed marriages are cumulative and are far more frequent in the homes that are themselves mixed marriages than is true the other way around. Children marry out of their groups far more frequently when their parents' marriage itself was either mixed or indifferent in its origin.

Thirdly, family and church and close friends have far less control than formerly. "But I love him" is the answer to any objections that a church or home may make today. In some of the three-generation studies that have been going on, parents today are found to disapprove more frequently their daughters' boyfriends than was true one generation or two generations ago. This is true partly because parents apparently have less influence today and also because they are more frequently concerned about some of these mixed marriage threats to their young people.

What's the matter with the mixed marriage that the teenager so frequently considers? Let us marshal our resources and look at our facts. Our young people are demanding them and have a right to straight answers. First of all, there's no question but what the mixed marriage is more instable than the marriage within the same faith or within the same socioeconomic cultural group. The mixed marriage far more frequently breaks up in divorce, separation, or annulment.

Secondly, we find more expectation of failure on the part of members of the family and close friends. If a youngster marries his own kind of person, with the approval of his church and his family, and then gets into the early marriage adjustments that are pretty much inevitable, his family—her family say, "Now work it out; it is all right. It is just one of these early marriage adjustments. This, too, will pass. Just go on back now and get busy at building your marriage." But if she married the man her family did not approve, who came from a different background, a different religious faith, and she goes home to Mama, Mama will say, "Oh, you poor darling. But then I told you that if you made a mixed marriage that it wouldn't work." This kind of social disapproval, this kind of expectation of failure that we understandably have, as far as the mixed marriage is concerned, only makes the job of working it out more complicated.

A third factor is that there is more difficulty in rearing children in meshing social and religious aspects of the two cultures when the two people do not see eye to eye and have literally built into them as personalities different ways of looking, feeling, and being concerned about the various aspects of child rearing.

Fourth is a factor that needs to be underlined in our own minds, as well as that of young people. That is, the mixed marriage is far more frequent among the impulsive, rebellious, immature youngsters who are making lunges for independence and who unconsciously, if not consciously, say, "I'll marry some impossible person. I'll show him, her, them, that I can't be pushed around. I am grown up, I am going to do something on my own." Mixed marriages are far more frequent among the very young and among the rebellious, impulsive youngsters.

The mixed marriage can and does work out in many cases, but it requires that both members of the pair be mature, responsible for their decisions, that they have adequate preparation, not only for marriage in general, but for their own particular marriage before the wedding takes place.

After the wedding the couple and their families need to learn to live with their differences constructively. In all of our emphasis on education for marriage we need to do far more than we have done thus far in helping our young people understand themselves, understand each other, and know how to find joy and fulfilment in the inevitable differences that they will continue to encounter, not only in their most intimate associations, but in their widening contacts throughout the world.

4

Mature Enough to Marry

The United States Bureau of the Census tells us that marriages today are taking place in larger numbers and at younger ages than ever before. In 1890 only 63 per cent of the population ever got married. In 1960 nine out of ten of us were married. In 1890 a man was in his twenty-seventh year before he married. Today young Joe, his grandson, is twenty-two and marries a girl who is barely twenty. Half of all our American girls are married by their twentieth birthdays.

In looking at teen-age marriages, as a great many researchers have in recent years, we find that most of our teen-age marriages are those of teen-age girls marrying older fellows. Nine out of ten of our high school marriages are those in which girls are marrying out-of-school or older boys. Why the increase in young marriages?

1. The first, and very possibly the most important, social reason is the relative affluence of present-day America. Thanks to the prosperity and high employment of recent years both bride and groom not only expect to work but usually do work until their family is established. During periods of depression, recession, and economic slowdown, the marriage age tends to be higher. As soon as times are good again, the number of marriages goes up. There's a very close relationship between economic prosperity and young age at marriage.

2. A second point of very real importance that is not widely

recognized is that parents today are more able and more willing to help the young couple in many substantial ways. We do a lot of face saving as we help these youngsters get established in marriage. We make generous gifts under the counter so the neighbors won't know. We help subsidize the first baby, contribute to the down payment on the house, help the youngsters get a new car, and do all kinds of things that older generations always have done, but we do it in a less obvious and more generous way today.

3. In the third place, there seems to be an increase in the general insecurity and loneliness in the uneasy world in which marriage rates continue to soar. Particularly in times of wartime economy and of general "floating anxiety," as the psychiatrists put it, marriage rates and young marriages increase during periods of social uneasiness.

4. Fourth is the increased amount of early dating (earlier than it used to be) , going steady at earlier ages, getting involved at earlier ages with marriage an inevitable next step. Courtship proceeds at a faster pace and at earlier ages than was the case a few generations ago.

5. Fifth, many of our young marriages are being forced by pregnancy. Estimates of the number differ by the various areas that have been studied. Dr. Harold Christensen of Purdue University goes to the records at the county courthouse in a given area and gets the date of the wedding and the date of the birth of the first baby. If the first baby is born seven months or less after the wedding he assumes that the baby was conceived before the wedding took place. There has been a very obvious increase in the number of these premarital pregnancies. The percentages not only vary by the area but also by the religious orientation, by the way.

6. Sixth is the idealization of marriage as a desirable adult status. The University of Chicago studies, *Growing Up in River City,* of all of the young people in one community from sixth grade on, found that those young people who felt that other doors for the future were closed, who were discouraged about

going on to college, who weren't doing well in school, whose own social adjustments were inadequate and felt left out, very frequently saw marriage as an easy way to get a quick status. If a girl felt she was a failure and could find any boy to marry her, at least now she had a little ring to give her a feeling of some importance. It was the same thing apparently for many of the boys. Marriage is a kind of instant status for a youngster who is discouraged in other areas. One of the reasons why some of these very young marriages work out so badly is that the very people who are least prepared for marriage are those who plunge into marriage most precipitately.

7. Seven, a point that is closely related but different is that the increase in young marriages is very definitely related to the increase in the number of unhappy homes, schools, and communities. As our schools and communities become much larger and more complex, the emphasis upon the individual decreases and far more of our young people fall through the net of our adult concern. Children from unhappy homes marry at younger ages than those from happier home situations.

8. Eighth is the chain reaction effect of young marriages, encouraging more young marriages within a given community. In some schools the vast majority of senior girls are already either engaged or married. It becomes such "the thing to do" that there is a disease the guidance people call "senior panic" among the girls. Such girls feel, "If you do not have your man, if you do not have your ring, if you are not already committed, you have missed the boat somehow in school." In many communities, getting married at young ages has attained almost epidemic proportions.

Some of our more probing studies of the individual factors within the persons themselves shed even further light on some of the contributing factors for young marriages. Dr. Burchinal's chapter in our *Sex Ways in Fact and Faith* reports research that finds: (1) Girls who marry young tend to be those who have mothers who married young. Young people identify with their own parents and tend to carry out the same pattern of life their parents have established for them. (2) The girls who marry young tend to be those who started dating at early ages. (3) They are the ones who began going steady at earlier ages (and with more individuals) and who began to go steady from an earlier point in their courtship period. (4) They have been in love a greater number of times. (5) They have known more close friends who also married young. Again there is a cumulative effect within the neighborhood. (6) They more frequently dated older men. The high school girl who goes with an out-of-school fellow, already established in some kind of job, is far more apt to marry before she finishes school than the girl who dates the high school boy about her own age, who is still in school and has aspirations beyond school. (7) Girls who marry young tend to be those who have low aspiration levels for themselves. They are not the girls who plan to go on to college, who seem themselves to have a future beyond "just being a housewife."

Early marrying youngsters tend to be those boys and girls who feel discouraged about themselves and as a rule have low aspiration levels. The girls who marry young usually marry the boys in the trades, in unskilled and semiskilled work, rather than those who have further educational plans, dreams, hopes, and vocational aspirations. The girl who marries young tends to marry the boy who is already established at some low-paying job with little future in it. He got it because it is all he can get after dropping out of school. This is an old familiar story which represents a great deal of human erosion in our society. Sensitive, socially aware persons recognize that it is intimately related to this young marriage problem.

Why be concerned about young marriage? First of all, because of its human development hazards. Erik Erikson and the other specialists in the field of human development have pointed out very vividly that with early domesticity you get a cutting off of the further development of the personality. Anthropologists have found in simple folk societies, where young people typically not only married young but had early sex experience, that the young people in those societies live out their lives on a relatively simple level of competence. If a boy can fish or throw a spear or weave a fishing net that is all that is required of him. If a girl can biologically bear a baby that the rest of the society will take care of, as happens in the simple folk society, that is all that is required of her. She is one of the society of women who take care of the children. This requires a much lower level of competence, a much lower level of personality development than is required and through which fulfilment comes in our society.

There seems to be little question but that early intimacy and early domesticity among teen-agers curtails the development of full personality potential. The individual becomes preoccupied in the creative and procreative aspects of life which all of us know have such terrific drive and central force. Therefore, that individual does not get the time or the chance to dream the long dreams, to think the big thoughts, to get exposed to art and music, the big ideas and the big social problems, and people different from himself. He or she does not get a chance to travel and to explore and to find out what the world is made of and know the kinds of people and the forces and attitudes and points of view that are present. He or she does not get the opportunity to develop as a full-fledged individual to the place of developing the very complex, intricate, marvelous capacity to love in its fullest sense.

This is the big reason why we advocate no premarital intercourse. This is the reason why young marriages should not be recommended in our society. But there is another reason too. This is that young marriages do break up in large numbers. They more often break in divorce, separation, and annulment than do those of more mature persons. All studies to date conclude that young marriages are not as stable as those of more mature persons.

Professor Judson T. Landis did a very interesting study comparing the age of marriage with divorce. He found that when both of the pair were under twenty, 20.2 per cent of them got divorced. When both of the pair were in the early twenties, from twenty to twenty-five years of age, only 10 per cent got divorced. When both of the pair were in their late twenties (twenty-six to thirty), 8.7 per cent divorced; and when both were over thirty when they married, 7.4 per cent divorced. Now if you draw a little graph for yourself, you find the big drop in divorce rate comes after age twenty at marriage. By the time most of our young people get into their twenties they have achieved enough maturity so that marriage can be assured of some permanence.

Why are young marriages so unstable? Because marriage is not child's play. It requires a very complex ability to carry responsibility and to settle down as a mature enough person to found a family. Young marriage is very frequently a lunge toward independence and freedom from control. Therefore, it tends to take place most frequently among the most rebellious, the most anarchistic, the least well-adjusted young people. "You can't push me around, I'll get married and show you I can run my own life" kind of attitude is adolescent rebellion at its most immature form. This lunge for independence oftentimes takes the form of a lunge into marriage.

The young married are often emotionally immature even though they may be sexually sophisticated. Human development findings are quite clear that sexual sophistication is related negatively to emotional maturity. The more emotionally mature a person is, the more responsible he is in his sexual life. Less emotional maturity is related significantly, clinically and statistically, to sexual irresponsibility, promiscuity, and general sophistication sexually.

Why are young marriages unsuccessful in terms of both permanence and happiness? Because young people have less opportunity to prepare themselves specifically for marriage and family, less opportunity to find out what marriage is all about, less opportunity to understand themselves and what it means to become a husband or wife, a mother or father, less opportunity to learn anything at all about what it is going to mean to become parents. Very possibly one of the reasons why children tend to be hard on marriage is that too few of our young people get specific education in what to expect of children, how to understand the process of child development, and what to anticipate as children's needs through the developmental cycles of childhood.

I shall never forget a young man I met on one of our college campuses, a freshman at the time, who was married and had a baby and who said, "I had no idea of what being married and having a baby would be like. As it is I fumbled along and almost lost out. My wife took the baby back to her folks and it wasn't until I took a course in family living that I knew what was the matter and what I had better do about it."

That came directly from a freshman in college who had married before he had finished high school. Or another one, this time a girl who with tears in her eyes and a sob in her voice said this, "I've just had no fun since I got married. I can't go to parties. I just don't feel right in school any more—or in any of the other school activities. I guess I thought he was the only one in the world. Oh, how mixed up can you get?"

These youngsters oftentimes recognize all too late that the problems of marriage are way beyond their anticipations. Marriage has been ballooned up in our romantic literature, in the very folklore that our young people breathe, as the answer to their problems. Indeed it is not. It brings its own problems, its own adjustments.

What are these pressures on young people that tend to break those marriages made too early, too prematurely, too precipitantly? What happens? What are the pressures and problems of young marriages? First of all are the economic problems and pressures. Fifty per cent of the husbands and 80 per cent of the wives, who married before they were twenty, list money problems as almost insoluble in their marriage, for understandable reasons. These couples marrying at young ages have less money and more unemployment. This is the very part of our population that finds it most difficult to get jobs because they have no saleable skills. Our technology is becoming more and more complicated, requiring more and more education, and more and more specialized training. The youngsters who drop out of school to get married before they have given themselves the advantage of education find it most difficult to get a decent job and hold it. They have less money, more unemployment, less of an educational base, and the wife is poorly prepared to help. About all she can do is get a job as a waitress, or pounding somebody's typewriter, or other more or less dead-end jobs.

A second pressure on these young marriages is that of housing. Paul Glick in the book, *American Families,* points out from census figures that a large number of these young couples live with their folks even though our culture says "no roof is big enough for two families." Just a couple of years ago one of our large state universities found that 66 per cent of their young married couples were living with one or the other set of parents. That is higher than you find in some other places. Nationally, about a third of these young couples bunk in with Mom and Dad. This is a very real problem, and it may be a real disappointment.

I talked with a young bride not too many years ago who felt this keenly. She said, "Here I am married eighteen months and I don't even own an egg beater." She had grown up with a *Ladies' Home Journal* bride kind of picture in her head that when you get married you hit the jackpot. She expected upon marriage a nice little home with roses over the porch, a nice little garage with at least one car, and a nice little model kitchen with electrical equipment. Her parents probably were married twenty or twenty-five years before they had this picture, today portrayed as coming with marriage.

Young marriages have in-law problems. They have three times as many in-law problems as we find among more mature couples. Why? Because parents more frequently disapprove of the young marriage and, therefore, are on the lookout for trouble. The kind of attitude, "All right, I told you you were going to run into trouble—dropping out of school and getting married when you did. Don't come running back to me. You've made your bed—now lie in it," is not uncommon.

The more mature marriage that parents approve tends to get a great deal more support from the parents on both sides of the family than the immature one. With the young marriage the parents have to give more assistance, bail the kids out more frequently, and become annoyed and feel imposed upon. They may direct their annoyance at the opposite member of the young pair. If it is the daughter, "Why doesn't that young man get going? When I was his age I was out doing three jobs." Annoyance and disappointment on the part of parents increase the concern from the parents' point of view which the young people, in turn, interpret as interference.

The young married couples themselves say that their in-laws interfere and tend to reject the married partner far more frequently than is the case when the couple is more mature. Some seven-tenths of young wives with in-law problems did not get support from their husbands who sided with their parents in conflict. This again is a mark of immaturity. When the pressure gets on and the boy finds himself being attacked by a young wife for some marital problem or adjustment that they haven't worked out yet, his mom is apt to say, "Oh, you poor dear." He runs to Mom for solace and comfort, because he has not emancipated himself enough to work these things out, man to man, with his wife. This takes a great deal of maturity as any of us as married people know from personal as well as professional experience. In-law problems are greater by far among people who marry young than those who marry at a more mature age.

Another hazard is the social pressures. Three times as many young brides as mature ones complain of their husbands not settling down. Young husbands run around much more than do more mature men. "He is out bowling with the boys." "He leaves right after supper and I have no idea where he goes." "He is still chasing around" is the kind of complaint that very frequently comes from the young wife.

The young mother oftentimes finds that the constant care of a baby ties her down, making it impossible even to get out and do the shopping, not to mention the fellowship with the girls that she has always enjoyed. She feels closed off from normal social outlets. Here the girl is stuck twenty-four hours a day, seven days a week, with an irresponsible husband who is off goodness knows where; so she parks the baby any place she can and tears off whenever possible. Irresponsible, sure, because she is not ready for this kind of responsibility.

What is happening to the whole generation of babies coming from this large number of young marriages where neither mother nor father are really ready to give the kind of love, the kind of care, and develop the kind of home that we know babies need to grow up in? This problem is going to continue to increase unless somehow we can be more effective in preparing youngsters for marriage.

Studies have been done among young couples up to five years after they were married. Researchers ask the question, "If you had it to do all over again, would you marry when you did?" The most frequent reply is, "Well, I probably would, but I wouldn't advise anybody else to. It's just too rough."

What do we mean—mature enough to marry? Generally speaking, figures show that those persons who marry after they get into their twenties do a better job in marriage. Birthdays are not the only measure of either age or youth. What does maturity for marriage look like? First of all, mature enough to have established a sense of personal identity, to have discovered oneself and to have developed a direction for one's life that offers promise for the future. Mature enough to have developed a sense of personal identity with a sense of the direction that one's future will take.

Second, mature enough to be ready to settle down with one person exclusively, with responsibility. Third, grown up enough to have outgrown childish dependence upon parents or adolescent independence thrusts to the place where one is ready for interdependence with husband or wife. Fourth, a person is mature enough to marry when he or she is ready to love and to be loved deeply and fully as a whole person. The kind of love that takes time to mature does not blossom overnight, even in a relationship between mature persons.

Fifth, education sufficient for a full life as a man or woman both in and outside the home. There should have been enough education before marriage to kindle the love of learning in both of the pair so they will both keep on with their education afterwards. If the young person has had enough education to want to keep on afterwards, he will marry the kind of person who plans to continue learning. The girl will find, then, that her husband supports her if she wants to take a college course along the way, enjoying every minute of it, because there had been enough educational background to build on and to give a feeling of fulfilment and satisfaction, excitement and growth.

It is this love of growth that probably more than anything else is a measure of maturity. Education is important for a full life. So, we advise youth—prepare for what marriage involves. Become ready to assume the roles and even enjoy the privileges of marriage. Know what it means to become a husband, what it means to become a wife. Learn what will be expected and enough of the skills to carry on with some competence as a married partner, as a parent, as a householder, as a homemaker. Develop enough skills now to give some competence and satisfaction in life later.

Those of us who have anything to do with children in the full twenty years of the first two decades of life need to constantly recognize that more important than preaching, more important than scolding, more important than reminding is encouraging young people to develop those facets of themselves that have promise. As we can show a youngster from the very earliest days our pleasure, our pride, our admiration for something that he is or does or is capable of, we inspire him to continue growing. When we whittle down or nag too loudly, too frequently—all we do is increase the sense of guilt and shame and disappointment and self-abasement that is not in the line of growth.

Second, we can help young people find meanings to life by helping them develop the skills, the attitudes, and the values that put them in tune with the wonders of life around them and within themselves. And next, we can specifically, step by step, prepare young people for marriage early enough to give a solid foundation. This is especially important for those who might rush precipitantly into marriage unless they get some insight early enough.

In many of our high schools where the young marriages are taking place in largest numbers, the course in marriage is saved for the senior year when the youngsters that are going to marry have already dropped out. Our challenge is in providing graduated opportunities for becoming increasingly socially, emotionally, and spiritually alive. Now this is a big order. It implies taking a new look at our program, at our curricula, at the material we have been writing for young people, and the very approach that we make to them personally.

I have been accused of being an optimist. I'm not. I'm concerned, because I see mankind around the world investing literally billions in implements of destruction, and I see even our most concerned persons giving but a very small fraction of their time, their energy, and their money to trying to tap the precious power in the human spirit. That is the only antidote I know to the rampant anxiety and hate that are abroad today. It is only as we can call concerned persons like you to take a new look at what we might be doing in developing people, and the homes of tomorrow, that our future can be secure.

5

Families in Our Times

It is said that when our first parents were leaving the Garden of Eden in disgrace Adam turned to his wife Eve and, by way of making conversation in their rather distressing situation, remarked, "My dear, we are living in an age of transition."

It could certainly be said that the American family is passing through a time of transition. We are experiencing today enormous social and cultural changes. There has been no comparable era in human history. And we are seeing families—your family and mine—struggling with those enormous changes and trying to keep their equilibrium in the process.

I find that, when you are among Baptists, you are always on very sure ground if you start with the Bible. This I intend to do. When we look at the family in the Bible, we find that it belongs to a particular structure or framework of family life that is very recognizable. We call it the *patriarchal* family. The Bible family is almost a classical illustration of the patriarchal family.

I do not myself think that for this reason we need say that the patriarchal family represents God's ultimate purpose for the human family. We would not necessarily be better Christians if we tried to conform to the particular cultural factors that were present in Bible times. I don't think it would be any more pleasing to God if we went around wearing sandals and long flowing white robes, and lived in houses built of mud with flat roofs, than by living in the way we do. Therefore, I do not think it follows that the particular structure of the family that we find in the Bible is God's final purpose for the family.

What is the mark of the Christian family is not its particular form or structure. Of course, some forms of the family, such as polygamy, would be wholly unacceptable to Christian principles. But leaving those out of account, what makes a family Christian is the quality of life and of relationships that go on within a family—whatever its particular form or structure may happen to be. What is important is the degree to which the Christian virtues and the Christian graces are lived out among the members of the family.

However, it happened to be the patriarchal family that characterized Bible times. And the patriarchal family has been found widespread in almost all the great human cultures. We can trace it back in an unbroken line to the Sumerian civilization of about 4000 B.C. It is the family in which the father is the authority figure, the big boss. The family structure is held together by a complex balance between authority on the one hand and obedience on the other. You find this at three levels: (1) the authority of the senior family—the people we call the in-laws—together over the young couple, the junior family; (2) the authority of the husband over the wife; and (3) the authority of the parent over the child. Authority and obedience.

This kind of family system has been rooted in land tenure. It has been an immensely strong, unyielding family system, which has had tremendous endurance. It has served, during a vast span of human history, extraordinarily well. But when, nearly two hundred years ago in my native Britain, an event took place which we now describe as the Industrial Revolution, the doom of the patriarchal family system was finally sounded. The people began to leave the land and come up to the cities. The factories were thrown up—those "dark satanic mills," as William Blake called them. And soon we began to see the old family system breaking up and disintegrating. This process has gone on ever since with the rapid increase of industrialization and organization all over the world.

It was Professor Whitehead, one of our great British social philosophers, who once said that whereas before the Industrial Revolution the quality of an institution that gave it permanence was *stability,* since the Industrial Revolution the quality of an institution that has given it permanence has been *flexibility* and *adaptability.* The patriarchal family did not have flexibility or adaptability. Consequently, under the impact of rapid social change, caught up in an enormous cultural mutation, the patriarchal family on every hand is dead or dying, decaying and disintegrating. If you were to draw a map of the world, and sketch in on that map the areas where industrialization and urbanization have gone farthest, you would pretty accurately indicate those parts of the world where the patriarchal family is in its most advanced stages of decay.

As we contemplate today the widespread collapse and disintegration of the patriarchal family, it certainly looks very disturbing to us. It can easily be mistaken for the breakdown of the family as an institution. Many of us have so interpreted it. We have felt despondent at times about the things that are going on around us. We have wrung our hands and cried: "Whatever is happening to family life?" And there *are* some disturbing things happening to family life, apart from this particular change. But I do believe that if we understand more clearly what this change is, we can take a more intelligent, and I think a more optimistic, view of what is happening in our time. At least we can grasp what is happening more clearly; and that, I think, is of quite considerable importance.

What I believe is that, just as the old legendary bird, the phoenix, died in an outburst of flames and left behind it a heap of ashes out of which, miraculously, there arose a new phoenix, with new life and new vitality, so from the dying, disintegrating ruins of the old patriarchal family system there is already emerging a new kind of family system to take its place. And this new kind of family system fits more comfortably into the new life of the new world into which, whether we like it or not, we are all being carried by the relentless wheels of onward progress.

The new form of the family, which you have all heard described by our sociologists as the "democratic family," is the one to which I wish to devote attention in the remaining discussion. I want to indicate what shape it is taking, and what tasks and challenges it presents to us. I shall summarize what I say under four key words. They are all words that you will like. They are words that are democratic, that represent values you believe in. The four words are *freedom, independence, equality,* and *fulfilment.*

1. First, *freedom.* This is a word that we love. We say that we will fight and live and die and work for freedom. Yet freedom is really a very dangerous thing unless it is rightly used.

What perhaps we don't see as clearly as we should sometimes is that here in this Western culture of ours we have staked everything on a tremendous principle. During most of human history, and still in most parts of the world today, the belief has been that human society will only function properly when a group of special people, who understand and are knowledgeable and superior, decide what the others will do, and tell them what to do, and keep them in their place. This has been the pattern of human culture during most of human history.

We have staked our destiny on the concept that human society will work best if we give to every individual the maximum degree of freedom and responsibility, the autonomy and self-realization that he can take. I believe this is a valid, Christian principle, because it rests upon the concept of the unlimited worth of the individual in the sight of God and in the sight of his fellowmen. This is our new concept of democracy. The world has never put it to the test before on the scale on which we are embarked on testing it today. We don't even yet know whether our experiment is going to succeed. But we believe in it, and we are pledged to see it through.

Of course, this concept of freedom applies within the family, too. One of the points at which it manifests itself most strikingly is that our young people nowadays assert the almost absolute right to choose their marriage partners as they see fit. This is of

course a new idea. During most of human history, and for most
people in the world until very recently, marriage partners were
chosen for them by their parents or by a professional go-
between. Indeed, until China went Communist about a decade
ago, it was still true that more than half of the human race went
into marriages under arrangement.

I remember being in a little town in India, and there was a
lot of talk about something that had happened the previous day.
Two young men were going out in the customary manner, each
with his retinue of friends and followers, to claim their brides.
The particular professional go-between who had arranged both
of these marriages had somehow got his instructions mixed up,
and the two young men were headed straight to the wrong
homes. Well, they managed to straighten it out by sending
couriers to intercept them and give them the correct addresses.
But the point of the story is that it would have been at least
theoretically possible for these young men to have gone to the
wrong addresses and collected and married the wrong girls!
They wouldn't have been any wiser, because they had never
seen the girls before. Indeed, there have been human cultures in
which the young man did not even look upon the face of his
bride until he had married her. Then and only then he was
allowed to lift the veil and see his wife's face!

When I say that our Western democratic concept is different,
this is an understatement! Our young people today have taken
to themselves the right to date and to fall in love and to get
married. Sometimes they consult their parents, sometimes their
parents feel that they can make a feeble protest; but most of
them, I find, feel that they pretty well have to go along with
whatever the choice is.

This is, of course, an act of faith in the capacity of young
people to exercise responsible judgment. But are they always
exercising responsible judgment? Unfortunately no. Most of
them are trying to be as responsible as they can, but some are
not always succeeding, as we see from this high rate of breakdown of early marriage about which we have been hearing.

I remember speaking about marriage at a meeting once, and a girl came up to me afterwards and said, "I'm going steady with a young man, and he is just the right young man for me!" I said, "I'm glad you are so sure about it. Tell me, how do you know that he is just the right young man for you?" A kind of rhapsodic look came into her face, and she said, "Well, you see, every time I meet that young man I just tremble all over like a plate of Jell-O!"

It was perhaps something of an achievement in this young man to cause this kind of emotional agitation in this girl every time that she met him. But really, really now, what did this have to do with the capacity of these two young people to live together in the most complex and intimate and demanding of all human relationships for half a century? Not really very much.

What was the girl doing? Faced with a situation in which she had to make a choice, and not having any clearly defined rational criteria on the basis of which to make the choice, she just did what we all do. She trusted her emotions. But if some of us had to make choices like that, where would we be? Suppose you went to pick a car out of the used car lot, and you knew nothing about what went on underneath the hood or inside the works, and you looked at them all and said, "Oh, I'll have that pretty red one." Would this be a good way of choosing a car? Of course it wouldn't. But you see, if young people have to make their choices with no clearly defined concept of what marriage is all about and what it takes to build a good partnership—these known and established scientific facts—if they do not have this information, who can blame them if they follow their emotional hunches? It is what we all do in the absence of something better.

So we have today a new situation that demands a new kind of solution. People will say that our grandfathers and grandmothers didn't need courses on education and preparation for marriage. Of course they didn't. They didn't have to carry the burden of this tremendously responsible choice.

We as parents cannot do as Eastern parents do. Some of them make it the supreme achievement of their lives to find good partners for their sons and daughters. But whether we think we could do it or not, we are not able to search the town in order to find the most suitable young man or young woman to be the husband or wife of our beloved daughter or son. This power is no longer ours. But we are not thereby exonerated from responsibility.

In the new situation of the new times to which we belong, we are as responsible as parents ever were. However, we have to discharge our responsibilities in a new way, by seeing to it that our young people as they grow up get the right sort of teaching, the right sort of guidance, and the right sort of preparation, so that if they do have to make their own choices in freedom, they make those choices with the light of knowledge in their eyes. A new situation requires a new solution.

2. The second word is *independence*. This is really an extension of freedom. Our young people are not only saying they will choose their mates for themselves in freedom. They are also saying, "Yes, and when we *have* chosen our mates, we will live with them without interference." When they talk about interference they mean relatives, and particularly, they mean in-laws! So they say, "Outlaw the in-laws!"

Who are those monstrous in-laws that we hear all those terrible things about? They are none other than the loving, devoted fathers and mothers who want with all their hearts the best for their children that their children can have. But why are they thus condemned? Not, I think, because young people don't love their parents as much now as they ever did.

Of course, nowadays they are not afraid of their parents, so they are franker about their sentiments than we were when we were younger; but I think they love their parents just as much as we did ours. The protest against in-law interference is a protest against the system of authority and obedience. It is the over-throw of the old hierarchical system, and when the young people seem to be attacking their parents, they are really attacking the system, and the parents have to bear the brunt of the attack on the system.

So they say, "Outlaw the in-laws." Yes, but in-laws have their uses. They make wonderful babysitters, and they are a very present help in trouble when the bank balance goes in the red, and they do all kinds of other things. One of the things that they have traditionally done is to step in when the marriage runs into trouble.

I remember seeing a very striking illustration of this in England. A young Jewish couple came to me. They talked about their troubles, and I thought that this was a routine marriage counseling job. But I soon found that it was going to be different. I discovered that there was going to be a grand family council, at which parents on both sides, all surviving grandparents, and miscellaneous uncles and aunts, plus the rabbi—and myself as the expert consultant—were going to sit down and sort this thing out. I was a little skeptical at first, but it was a wonderful experience. It showed me how marital problems were handled in the old days in the family council. I must say they did a good job, and they did straighten the pair out.

But if you outlaw the in-laws, you can't call them in when you are in trouble to straighten out your difficulties. Anyway, our young people today are not of a mind to take their marital troubles to their parents. If they did, perhaps they would find that their parents are wiser than they think. But still, that's the way they look at it. So again, the new situation requires a new kind of remedy. When our young people are in marital difficulties today, there's no family council that can be called to straighten them out. So they look for the neutral and independent expert—that new person who has walked into the social scene whom we call the marriage counselor.

Maybe after all the marriage counselor, neutral and independent, trained and qualified, can do a better job than the parents, who in spite of all their desires to be objective are very much inclined to take the side of their own dear sons and daughters. So again the new situation requires a new solution.

3. The third word is *equality*. The first time I went to India, I was talking to a group of Indians about marriage counseling, and they said to me, "What is this marriage counseling?" "Tell me," I replied, "when husband and wife quarrel in your culture, what happens?" "Oh," they said, "it doesn't happen." I said, "I am not making myself clear. Let me try again. When the husband thinks one way and the wife thinks differently, so that they disagree, what happens?" They still said, "It doesn't happen." "Well," I said, "you are going to teach me something. Go ahead." They explained to me how, when the Indian girl is quite small, she is taught that the day will come when she will have a husband; and how she must look up to him, and regard him as perfect, because nothing he can do is wrong, and nothing he can say is wrong. It is Hindu doctrine, as you know, that an Indian woman cannot worship God directly. She worships God through the worship of her husband. So the Indians solved very neatly the clash of conflicting wills in marriage, by arranging that there should be only one boss, and that he should always be right.

In Africa you find something very similar. For some months I lived in Johannesburg, where I was visiting professor at the University of the Witwatersrand for a term. I remember looking out of the window once and seeing an African couple walking along the sidewalk. Now if you saw an American married couple walking along the sidewalk, they would be walking side by side, and if they were feeling very amorous they might even be walking arm in arm or hand in hand. But not so this African couple. The husband, dressed in a Western suit, with a hat tilted at a jaunty angle and a cigarette in his mouth, and carrying a cane, was walking along as if he owned the place. Behind him, at a respectful distance, there followed his little wife. In each hand she carried a suitcase that was obviously pretty full of luggage of one kind or another, and, with the grace and poise that are characteristic of the African woman, on her head she balanced a very heavy and old-fashioned sewing machine!

This is the African concept. On another occasion, out in

Zululand, I remember talking to a native family. They lived in a little straw house like a large beehive, with a little hole to crawl in. I asked them how they ate their meals, and then I said, "And, how do you arrange yourselves when you sleep?" The husband said, "I sleep over there," indicating the very farthest point from the door. I said, "Where do the children sleep?" And then, "And where does the wife sleep?" "Well," he said, "she lies across the doorway." I said, "Why is this?" "Well, you see," said the husband, "if in the night some marauder, or some wild beast should come, then that gives me time to wake up and find my spear!"

For most of human history, this has been the relationship of the man and the woman. Then 1893 came and all was changed. You know what happened in 1893, don't you? On those two little islands in the South Pacific? Well, in 1893 the New Zealanders gave women the vote. They surely started something, because it went like a chain reaction round the world, and now today there are only a very few countries where women *don't* have the vote. So the emancipation of women has come in all kinds of ways, until now we talk about men and women as equal. Indeed, we go further than that. A distinguished fellow country-man of mine, resident as I am in the United States, wrote a book a few years ago titled *The Natural Superiority of Women*.

So we hear the young people of today saying, "We are going to have a fifty-fifty marriage." Of course what they mean is equality in terms of opportunity and responsibility as persons. But what we don't always realize is that, while it may be a fine thing to co-operate equally in the running of the home and the managing of the family, this is a far more difficult pattern to handle than to follow an established traditional blueprint handed down from previous generations. What it means is that marriage is much more difficult today, and because marriage is much more difficult a lot of people are just not going to manage to get through, unless we do a much better job of preparing them beforehand, and standing by to help them when they run into troubles that may engulf them overwhelmingly afterwards.

Today we are not only talking about equality between husband and wife, but we are talking also about equality between parent and child. When I was a boy in Scotland they used to say, "Little children should be seen and not heard." And this was the way it was. If we were privileged to sit at dinner when there was company, "Yes" and "No," and "Please pass the salt" was all that we were permitted to say. Beyond that, we had to sit in awe-struck silence, drinking in the words of wisdom that poured from the lips of our "elders and betters." But in the contemporary American home, the little children are seen and heard to such advantage that sometimes the grown-ups can't get a word in edgewise! Well, that's all right. But it's more difficult for the parents. An article in *Harper's Magazine* recently said that in the old days parents used to carry a big stick and go thump, thump. Nowadays parents go dainty, dainty, and carry a big book!

If we believe in this kind of free and co-operative interplay between parents and children, we have to face the fact that it is going to be much harder to work. It is far easier to say, "Go and see what Johnnie's doing and tell him not to," than to go yourself, and explain to him why he shouldn't be doing what he is doing, let him raise his objections, and meet them logically until finally you reach unanimity! This is far harder. This takes intelligent parenthood. This takes a knowledge of child development, so that you understand what Johnnie can do and can't do at his present stage of development. Only this way can we have the kind of free-flowing relationships within the family that have such dynamic potentialities. We have to have people who are much better educated for marriage and parenthood, and people who understand the need to seek help when things get so confused that they just can't cope any more.

4. Finally, we come to the word *fulfilment*. In the old days, marriage was a duty. You married because it was expected of you. It was a social duty, it was a civic duty, it was a religious duty to marry. When you went into marriage, nobody was very much concerned about whether you would be happy or not. If

you found happiness together, this was a nice bonus that you could be thankful for; if you were not happy together, you went on and did your duty just the same. I remember asking in India about what happened when life became really intolerable in marriage for the wife. They calmly told me that the proper thing for her to do was to commit suicide! This has been true in other Eastern countries as well. There is no way out. You grin and bear it. Happiness is a by-product that may come your way or may not. But marriage and raising a family is a duty.

For us in the West, the emphasis has shifted. We have turned it all upside down, and *we* say we marry because we are seeking fulfilment, seeking happiness. I talked to the editor of an American magazine some years ago about some articles that I might write for him. In the course of our conversation I said, "Have you ever carried in your magazine an article on how to adjust to a disappointing marriage?" He said, "No, I never have, and I don't think I ever will." He went on, "The American people don't believe that you have to adjust to a disappointing marriage. They believe that if your marriage is disappointing, the sensible thing to do is to get divorced and try again with somebody else, and hope that you will do better next time." I don't know how far he really represented the American people. I don't think he did, but there certainly are *some* people in the United States who feel that way about marriage. And about four hundred thousand couples every year get out of marriage, hoping to do better next time.

What this really means is that the great drive to the divorce court is based on idealism. It is idealism about marriage that is driving these people, in the hope and expectation that they will do better next time, because they have been persuaded that marriage should bring them happiness, should bring them fulfilment. Is it wrong to believe that? I believe not. Am I to judge them? I have found rich, deep, and lasting happiness and fulfilment in my marriage, and I believe that it was God's purpose that people should be happy in marriage.

I have been working with people in second marriages, and I

have been shaken to discover that many of them succeed in the second marriage only because they put into it a drive, a persistence, and a determination that somehow they just didn't have the first time. It took the collapse of one marriage and the entry into another marriage to teach them at last what marriage is all about. My friends, that is a very costly way of providing education for marriage in our culture.

You see, the trouble is that the drive of the idealism is misapplied. What we have not really shown people is that marriage is like everything else in human life. You get the rewards by working for them. This is not a garden already cultivated in which you take your ease. It often takes blood and sweat and tears and toil to build a good marriage, just as it does to build anything else that is good, lasting, and worthwhile. But somehow we have not been able to get this over.

So we must realize that, in our day and age, the family has staked its all on the belief that it can work out creatively these interpersonal relationships that bring happiness and fulfilment. What this means is that we cannot hold families together any longer by external coercion. They will hold together only by internal cohesion, and this means that we must give them preparation and give them guidance and give them help when they need it.

Now let me sum up. I have been reminding you, and you knew it already, that we are passing through a tremendously critical point in world history, in which everything is changing and we are on a great moving conveyor belt. I have tried to focus this tremendous cultural change in terms of what it is doing to the family. We have seen that, because families today are staking everything on the quest for good interpersonal relationships, the family has become much less stable. Yet, at the same time, the potentialities for good family life are greater for more people than they have ever been before.

This involves, I believe, a tremendous challenge for Christian people. Because families in our times have committed themselves to the achievement of good, harmonious, creative, interpersonal relationships, they are starkly confronted with the age-old problem that has faced the whole of human history—how can people who are different live together harmoniously and happily and peacefully? This has always been an important problem, but today it has become a problem so vital that our very survival depends upon it.

What then is the answer? How *can* people live together in harmony in close relationships? Does technology provide the answer? I don't think so. It helps, but it doesn't have the answer. Does behavioral science provide the answer? It helps us quite a lot, but I still don't think it provides the answer.

I cannot escape the conviction that the answer to this question is a religious answer. As Christians we have made the claim that there is a power that we can claim that can root out the deeply embedded selfishness and egotism within us, set us free to love creatively and redemptively, and in forgiveness and compassion and understanding enable us to live at peace with other people. We have said that this is true. We live at a point in the world's history at which we will be called upon to *demonstrate* that this is true, for this is the secret that men and women are looking for and staking everything on finding.

The challenge that confronts us today is to show the world what family life at its truest, deepest, and best can really be when the love of God is poured out in human lives, so that husbands and wives, parents and children are able—forbearing, forgiving, supporting, redeeming, and helping—to live together in harmony and in unity. This is the challenge that faces us. This is the task to which we are irrevocably committed. This is the witness that with God's help we are called upon to make to families in our times.

6

The
Nucleus of Family Life:
Marriage

In the long history of the Christian church there have been, in each succeeding generation, opportunities and challenges that have been relevant to the times. I believe that the present era is one in which the church is particularly involved in thinking and witnessing and working in the field of the Christian family—a field very sadly neglected throughout most of the history of Christendom.

My procedure, as you are aware, has been to divide this subject into three sections, beginning first with marriage, going on next to parenthood, and then talking about the family in its social environment. I hope in that way to catch most of the important issues, but I certainly am aware that I will not catch all of them. This is a vast subject, and even the generous allocation of space hardly suffices to cope with what is essential. I propose in each chapter to try first to indicate what the Bible has to say about the subject in question, and then to move on up to our modern complicated world and discuss some of the issues of our time. As I have indicated, I will have to be selective, and some issues that may seem to you to be of great importance will be left out.

It was Edward Westermarck, the great sociologist and anthropologist, in his monumental three-volume work, *The History of Human Marriage,* which has never been equaled—let alone surpassed, who established to everybody's satisfaction (except a few of his bitter opponents) that marriage is a universal human institution. In those three volumes of vast scholarship (completed, incidentally, by the time he was twenty-eight years of age; and incidentally, also, Westermarck himself never married) he combed out all available knowledge about all known human societies and proved that no stable, continuing, settled human society has been without the institution of marriage in some shape or form.

Westermarck demonstrated also, of course, that the institution of marriage has in fact existed in a great many shapes and forms. But I think we can take it as being broadly accepted that the human institution of marriage exists for three great basic purposes. These three purposes appear, in one form or another, in the preamble to most Christian marriage services.

1. First, marriage exists in order that children may be born and raised under the conditions best calculated to minister to their need to develop into mature and effective adults within their own particular culture. We have never found any substitute for a good father, mother, and child relationship.

2. Second, marriage exists within the complexity of human culture to keep the urgent and dynamic impulse of sex under some kind of control, so that instead of being, as it can be, a very disruptive and damaging force within society, it is channeled to become a creative and cohesive force within society. Again, human experience testifies very widely that outside of marriage sex can achieve great havoc in human relationships.

3. Third, marriage exists in order to make it possible for the unique relationship between a man and a woman, different from each other and complementary to each other, to develop in fulness and to achieve its greatest fruition. Man and woman friendships can be very rich and very highly developed outside marriage, but only within a lifetime of living together and sharing together can this unique comradeship come to its full fruition.

These then have been the three main purposes of marriage. In different cultures the stress has been on different elements, and perhaps the third element has had relatively little stress until our own times. But these are the purposes for which marriage has apparently been ordained by God, and which it has in one way or another sought to fulfil.

We as Christians accept these purposes of marriage, because they belong to the "order of creation," as we sometimes call it. They belong to everybody. But we go further, and we declare as Christians that in order that this fundamental order of creation shall be met, there are certain rules about marriage that have to be honored. Within our Christian fellowship there are three of these that are fundamental as we see it.

1. The first is *monogamy*. We believe as Christians that although multiple marriage has existed widely in many cultures, and still does, yet in order to fulfil completely God's purpose, marriage should be a relationship between one man and one woman.

2. Second, *fidelity*. We believe that the marriage relationship lays upon husband and wife a solemn moral obligation to be faithful to each other, sexually and otherwise, while the relationship continues.

3. Third, we believe that marriage should be *a lifelong commitment*. I am avoiding the term indissolubility, which is a Roman Catholic term and open to some question. But the concept that marriage should be a commitment of husband and wife, so long as they both shall live, is a Christian principle governing marriage.

As Christians, we believe that by keeping these rules we shall enable the three great aims of marriage to be best furthered. Of course, these principles may be derived from the Bible.

The Bible begins with the story of creation, and as part of the ordering of human life in the world that God made, we read that he ordained marriage. There isn't a lot said about the ordination of marriage, but what is said is very much to the point. In what is said there are three words used that are of particular significance in our deriving from that early Bible story the nature of marriage.

1. The first word is "flesh"—"they shall be one flesh" (Gen. 2:24). Marriage is a relationship rooted in biology, rooted in sex. If there were no sex, there would not need to be any marriage. Therefore, we have always believed that the sex relationship is the foundation of marriage, because the sex relationship is what gives marriage its peculiar and exclusive nature, as distinct from all other human relationships we know. And for that same reason, when the flesh is done away by the death of one of the partners, we believe as Christians that the marriage is terminated. Not all people believe that. Hindu marriage is perpetual. The Mormons also have a concept of perpetual marriage. But we believe that marriage is a relationship of the flesh, and we can support that from what Jesus said later—that in heaven "they neither marry, nor are given in marriage" (Matt. 22:30). So marriage is rooted in the flesh.

2. The second word in Genesis is the word "fruitful." "Be fruitful, and multiply" (1:28). Here we see the end of marriage that we have already looked at—the provision of a suitable setting or framework in which the child, as he grows up, is given the protection and guidance he needs.

3. The third important word is the word "one." "They shall be one flesh." This is the "unitive" concept of marriage, long neglected throughout Christian history. It has been brought into prominence and given significance, particularly in our time, by the brilliant theological insight of Sherwin Bailey, the Anglican theologian who, I think, has established the most significant breakthrough of our time in theological thinking about marriage.

These concepts of marriage which I have outlined very briefly were Hebrew concepts. They were given from the beginning, and the Hebrew people tried very hard to uphold them and succeeded to a praiseworthy extent. I know that you can go back to the Old Testament and find some aspects of sex life and of marriage that don't appear to be very creditable, but the Old Testament is giving us an account of the story of a people trying to follow faithfully the commands that God gave them, and failing, as we are failing in our times, sometimes to follow faithfully.

Nevertheless, I think that the Hebrew people, with a remarkable degree of fidelity, held fast, at least in their thinking and in their aspiring and in their idealism, to the fundamental concepts of marriage which had been given to them by God. Polygamy certainly we find, and we find it for a significant reason that I will come back to later. Divorce we also find. But when you compare the standards of marriage and family life of the Hebrews with the standards of the other cultures in the midst of which they lived, theirs is a very creditable performance—quite as creditable, I think, as the performance of Christian churches in our current American culture, which involves some factors that are far from Christian.

When we come to the New Testament, we find that there is little said about marriage except to reaffirm what had already been set forth. Jesus reaffirmed and gave his blessing and approval to the story in the Old Testament of the ordination of marriage and the family. He repeated the very words. In addition to that he said only two significant things by way of emphasis. On the one hand he said that for Christians, marriage, if they enter it, must be taken very seriously. He said this over against the rather loose ideas of divorce that were quite widespread in his time, especially as promulgated by the rabbinic school of Hillel. He said, "If you marry, you will go into a deep commitment."

I think it would be fruitless for us to engage in any lengthy discussion concerning what the New Testament teaches exactly about divorce. Biblical scholars have argued this back and forth for generations. Yet the purport of the teaching of the New Testament is pretty clear. I think that when you are trying to reconcile the Matthean exception, which allows divorce only on the ground of adultery, with the versions in the other Gospels, which do not allow divorce for any ground at all, it is pretty clear that, taking the Bible literally, the teaching is that divorce is not permitted at all. In that respect I think that the Roman

Catholic Church has faithfully followed the literal teaching of the Bible.

However, I believe, and I am sure you believe with me, that the literal teaching of the Bible can get us very far astray, unless we bring to bear upon every particular item of teaching the total impact of the whole atmosphere and character of the Bible truth. John Wesley once said that a man can wrest the Scripture to his destruction. And when you look at the total character of Christian truth, all that Jesus said about compassion and forgiveness, and all that he said about the primacy of the inward things above the external institutions, then I think we may say that the letter is not the last word, as the Roman Catholics have taken it to be. There is some place for divorce, in spite of the fact that as an ideal and as an objective the Christian teaching denies the right of divorce. This is a highly controversial question, and you can discuss it among yourselves. I have given you my interpretation for what it is worth.

First, then, Jesus said that if you do marry you must take it very seriously. None of us is in any doubt that the intention in a Christian marriage is that it shall be a lifelong commitment. And then, right at the other end of the continuum, Jesus said something very different. He said that although marriage is so vitally important—and it was so important for the Hebrews that there was a time when a young Hebrew might be brought before the court because he had not married, and asked why; yet there are some who, because of a high spiritual calling, may renounce all the joys and fulfilments God has offered them in love, in sex, in marriage, in parenthood, in order to fulfill that high spiritual calling.

This, of course, is what Jesus did himself. He declared that, despite the universal institution of marriage into which God has called us, there might be some who were called to celibacy. This, of course, started a lot of trouble. But, as Jesus declared, it is quite fair and quite reasonable that an individual Christian may be called to the life of celibacy in order to fulfil some high mission to which he feels he has a vocation.

Elsewhere in the New Testament, there is not much about marriage; but there is one thing that is of supreme importance. If anybody could be in any doubt whatever about the primacy of the Christian teaching about marriage as an institution ordained, blessed, and honored by God, he would have to confront the association that is declared in the New Testament between marriage and the relationship between Christ and the church. This lifts marriage to the highest plane, without any possibility of question or controversy. You find it in the Old Testament as well. You find the figure of marriage used to describe the patience and compassion and love of God with his wayward people Israel, a marriage in which the husband refuses to let go the wife who has failed and disgraced him.

Now, if we turn from the Bible to Christian history (and only a brief comment is relevant here), we find a sad story indeed. We find the intrusion into Christian thinking in the early centuries of alien elements. These came, I believe, from two directions —from the ascetic trends developed from the wave of Oriental philosophy that came across from the Far East, and from the concepts of Neoplatonism, which set flesh against spirit. These influences, I think, sadly contaminated the high and positive Christian thinking about marriage, and introduced an era in which many other factors played their part to put an emphasis on celibacy which was altogether out of proportion. The Roman Catholic Church through the long ages has, I think, erred sadly in its departure from simple Christian truth in this matter. This error found its consummation in the Council of Trent, where it was declared categorically that he who says that celibacy is not a higher spiritual state than marriage shall be anathema. This is still the official doctrinal teaching of the Roman Catholic Church today, and it is a dark denial of Christian truth as I understand it.

At the Reformation, Luther broke with the long dark tradition in which marriage and the family were relegated to a secondary level. He declared, in fact, what the Roman Catholic Church had never been willing to concede since the early centuries, that within the life of marriage and the family it was possible for men and women to find all the opportunity for the exercise of the Christian graces and of the Christian disciplines that they could find in the monastic cell. In other words, through the life of the family spiritual growth to its supreme heights can be attained, just as much as it can be attained by withdrawal from the world in the celibate life. This was the view of Luther who himself married. And so marriage was set free, within the Protestant tradition, to be restored to its original position.

However, it was not wholly or easily restored. The puritanical movements of Protestant history again and again swung Christian thinking back to the old negativism, the old fear and suspicion about sex and human love as being unspiritual. In a sense the battle is still being fought. But it is my belief (and this is one of the reasons why I consider conferences on family life to be of immense importance) that in this particular age of Christian history the opportunity has come at last for the full flowering of the Christian doctrine of marriage and the family.

Now let me turn from this background survey to the modern world in which we live. One of the things that has happened in our particular culture today is that traditional concepts of marriage have been turned upside down. This sounds like a rather dramatic statement, but I think I can substantiate it.

Throughout most of human history, the emphasis on marriage has been upon its utilitarian ends, and not upon the interpersonal relationship between husband and wife. That is to say, the unitive function in marriage, as Sherwin Bailey has termed it, has received very little attention, and it has always been placed second to the procreative function in marriage. This can be explained historically. It was a way of expressing the deep suspicion of sexuality that characterized much of early Christian thinking.

In our modern world, not through Christian initiative unfortunately but through secular insistence, the emphasis in marriage has been placed on the unitive function in such a way that the church can no longer ignore the challenge. An English Anglican theologian, William P. Wylie, has developed this concept in a very perceptive way. Of course, when you shift the focus in marriage from its utilitarian ends in producing children, maintaining the family line, and maintaining the continuity of the culture to the interpersonal achievement of unity, the *henosis,* as Sherwin Bailey has termed it, you get into a lot of trouble. Throughout most of human history, I suspect, people have known about this trouble. I think they have, therefore, deliberately avoided developing the interpersonal relationship in marriage, because they understood the explosive dangers that are latent in such development.

To make this clear to you, I want to take a little time to tell you an old story. It's a version of the creation story different from our own. It comes from India. It is a charming story. It contains a profound truth, and I think you will enjoy it.

In the beginning, when Twashtri came to the creation of woman, he found that he had exhausted his materials in the making of man, and that no solid elements were left. In this dilemma, after profound meditation, he did as follows: he took the rotundity of the moon, and the curves of the creepers, and the clinging of tendrils, and the trembling of grass, and the slenderness of the reed, and the bloom of flowers, and the lightness of leaves, and the tapering of the elephant's trunk, and the shy glances of deer, and the clustering of rows of bees, and the joyous gaiety of sunbeams, and the weeping of clouds, and the fickleness of the winds, and the timidity of the hare, and the vanity of the peacock, and the softness of the parrot's bosom, and the hardness of adamant, and the sweetness of honey, and the cruelty of the tiger, and the warm glow of the fire, and the coldness of snow, and the chattering of jays, and the cooing of the kokila, and the hypocrisy of the crane, and the fidelity of the chakrawaka, and compounding all these together he made woman and gave her to man.

But after one week, man came to him and said, "Lord, this creature that you have given me makes my life miserable. She chatters incessantly and teases beyond endurance and never leaves me alone; and she requires incessant attention and takes all my time up and cries about nothing and is always idle. And so I have come to give her back again, as I cannot live with her." So Twashtri said, "Very well," and he took her back.

Then after another week man came again to him and said, "Lord, I find that my life is very lonely since I gave you back that creature. I remember how she used to dance and sing to me and play with me and cling to me, and her laughter was music and she was beautiful to look at and soft to touch; so give her back to me again." So Twashtri said, "Very well," and he gave her back again.

And then, after only three days, man came back to him again and said, "Lord, I know not how it is, but after all I have come to the conclusion that she is more of a trouble than a pleasure to me. So please take her back again." But Twashtri said, "Out on you, be off! I will have no more of this. You must manage how you can." And man said, "But I cannot live with her," and Twashtri replied, "Neither could you live without her." And he turned his back on man, and went on with his work. Then man said, "What is to be done? For I cannot live either with her or without her."

There is a profound truth in that old story. And it would be equally true if it were told the other way round. When you bring man and woman together into a close and intimate relationship, you immediately create the problem of the clash of conflicting wills, which is understood, and has been well studied psychologically. I think that most human cultures have avoided this close interpersonal relationship in marriage because of the dangers, and they have done it in two ways.

First, by setting up a hierarchical distinction between the man and the woman, in which the man was considered to be an authoritative person and the woman had to be meek and submissive and obedient. That is to say, they declared that there was only one will in marriage, not two. And second, they have avoided the problem by sharply dividing the functions of the husband and the wife so that they didn't overlap and so that the couple didn't get into each other's hair.

What we have done in this day and age, for the first time in human history, has been to set the intimate interpersonal relationship in the center, as the goal of marriage, and to put the utilitarian considerations, which have always been in the center, out somewhere on the periphery. We'll come back to that later. But let me say now that I think this simple but profoundly significant fact is the root cause of most of our problems in marriage today. We have created a concept of marriage which offers a far higher potential in terms of interpersonal achievement and fulfilment than ever before; but in doing so we have made marriage much more difficult than ever before, and the result is that our culture is producing a very heavy casualty rate.

Now let me move from that fundamental statement to a very brief discussion of some of the problems that are plaguing us in our modern culture. I shall be able to do no more than identify a few of these problems and leave the discussion of them to you, if you so desire. I am going to mention five problems in marriage today, all of which concern us as Christians in one way or another.

1. The first problem is that of *early marriage*. We are confronted with the fact that young people are marrying earlier in our American culture than they have ever done since records were kept, and we must face the fact that the breakdown rate of these early marriages is disturbingly high. I think our concern about the early marriages is primarily because of a high breakdown rate which adds to our already swollen divorce figures.

Of course the Bible had no problem here, because in Bible times young people were married off quite soon after puberty. Our problem is that, in our complex modern culture, young people have to have so much education and preparation to assume the duties of adulthood that they are getting well on into life before they are qualified to earn a living and maintain a family. To my knowledge there's no fundamental objection to young marriage. If young marriages succeeded it would be all right. It may in fact be that young marriages could succeed better than we think they do, because I think that the statistics can be misleading.

It is my impression that the young people who are marrying early in our culture are not a true cross section of their age group. They are the young people who are insecure and disturbed, and who are trying to find in marriage a refuge for their insecurity and disturbance; or they are the young people who get involved in pregnancies and feel that there is no other way of meeting the situation than marriage. If these difficulties were overcome, it is not impossible that we might have quite successful young marriages. This is not, therefore, an ultimate problem, but it is a rather disturbing immediate one for us.

2. The second problem of our time is what I call *unreasonable expectations of marriage*. The concepts that so many young people have today of what marriage is going to bring to them are so much out of relation to reality that they are doomed to disappointment and unfulfilment from the very start. I sometimes think that in these days when the apocalyptic note has been somewhat hushed in religion, many people who used to pitch their aspirations toward bliss in heaven hereafter are nowadays focusing their aspirations toward bliss in marriage now. Marriage has become a sort of substitute for heaven in the aspirations of these people. Marriage is a pretty tough and rugged human institution; but it can't deliver at that level and, therefore, many people are going into marriage with expectations that are completely incapable of being fulfilled. They are, therefore, feeling frustrated and disturbed about their disappointment.

Tied up with this, of course, is the romantic complex. Someone has said that romantic love is the basis for marriage in our culture, and this is true. However, I do not myself believe that romantic love has the capacity for continuance. I do not think that a marriage can be based on romantic love. Romantic love is simply the tension, the longing, the yearning, and the aspiration created in persons who are powerfully sexually attracted but who are not able to fulfil their sexual desires. I think the whole testimony of human history makes this quite clear and plain. Romantic love, although it has some very beautiful and important spiritual overtones, is an episode that cannot last. Particularly, it is an episode that comes to an end inevitably when the lovers continue to satisfy their sexual needs. A sexual relationship sustained over a certain period inevitably leads to the withering away of romantic love. This is something that is not understood in our culture, with the result that many people today simply go from one marriage to another, working through the period of withering away of romantic love, and then, when that is ended, they seek another partner and start all over again.

Many a marriage, indeed, starts with the impetus of romantic love, but this passion, which is bound to wither and die, must be replaced in the process of association by conjugal love. This is based on a much wider range of much more enduring qualities, like the sense of shared experience, common interests, mutual comfort, dependency needs, compassion, and above all the altruistic love which is Christian *agape*. There isn't further time to expand this, but I am quite sure that this question of unreasonable expectation is one of the major problems of our time.

3. The third problem that I will mention in passing is the complicated problem of *role reversal* in marriage. The emancipation of women and the resulting concept of the equality of the sexes are fine ideals as long as we confine them to the equality and co-operation of men and women as persons in society. I think that is good Christian teaching. But when you get to the functional interaction of husband and wife in the relationship of marriage, where they are not equal but complementary to one another, then you get under any system of equality the problem of role reversal.

What we do see in our society today is a great many emancipated, defeminized women, and alongside them a great many bewildered and demasculinized men. One of the tragic illusions of our society today is that we are utterly confusing femininity with sexuality. Because of the demands of the American male, for complex reasons, American women, who are deeply aware in any case that they are not sure about their femininity, are trying to compensate for their bewilderment by overemphasizing their sexuality. They are, therefore, trying to respond to the desire of the American male to have an exotic woman; but the American male cannot be satisfied, and no male can be satisfied, with an exotic woman in the marriage relationship. And, therefore, there is a complex, self-defeating circle of forces at work here, producing role confusion. This is rather complex, and I am sorry that my treatment of it is so hurried.

4. The fourth problem is the *high rate of divorce and remarriage*. Divorce rates in the United States, as you know, are very high indeed. American divorces are twice those in the Soviet Union, four times those in Britain, six times those in Canada, and so on. These divorce rates are almost matched by remarriage rates. Seventy per cent of all divorced persons are remarried within four years, so what we really have is a rapid turnover rate in marriage partners. It's really what has been described as "seriatim polygamy," and is based, as I have indicated, very largely on these distorted expectations and this romantic illusion in which people feel they have to repeat the romantic experience over and over again to sustain the state of excitement that they find so satisfying.

This is a problem for us as Christians, because it goes contrary to our concept of marriage as a lifelong commitment, and this is something that we need to think about pretty seriously.

5. The fifth problem that I am going to mention is that of *the mixed marriage*. I just want to make one point about this. We have a great deal of evidence, statistical and clinical, that the chances of success of a mixed marriage are decidedly poorer than those of marriages between people of the same faith. We have, therefore, declared the mixed marriage to be rather an unmitigated evil. I cannot myself take this view. I think that mixed marriage has a place in God's purposes—not for everybody and perhaps only for a few. But I think that some mixed marriages have made a tremendous contribution toward breaking down walls of bitter misunderstanding and prejudice between different religious and cultural groups, and I believe that this has value. For some people, therefore, a mixed marriage may be a pioneer enterprise—a reaching out toward persons who think and feel differently, and breaking down these walls of partition

which, sooner or later, must be broken down—not only religiously, but nationally and in every other way, before the world can be a spiritual family.

I want to make one final point. There are, of course, many things that we can do to meet these problems of our time. We can do something about education and preparation for marriage. We can do something to provide marriage counseling services; and I could say a great deal about that, because I am heavily involved in setting up marriage counseling services here and elsewhere in the world. But I want now to focus your attention on another matter.

Let me put it in this way. As Christians, we are far too readily content with marriages that just manage to hold together, and we have failed rather badly to urge our people on to attain what I call the "higher reaches" of marriage. I see marriage as a venture in which two people climb heavenward together, and there is no limit to their progress in that enterprise. I think this is something that we have sadly neglected—the tremendous capacity for growth in a good marriage, and particularly in a Christian marriage.

This was what Luther asserted over against the view of the Roman Catholic Church—that marriage and the family offer a medium by which a man and a woman together can climb to great heights of spiritual growth. But how often do we think of marriage as an experience of climbing to great heights of spiritual growth? Often I have been with people when I have been going to give a talk about marriage, and they have said, "You won't mind if I don't come to your lecture tonight, will you? My marriage is all right." You see, the idea is that if my marriage is holding together, that's all that is required of me. The idea that I could learn something, the idea that my marriage could grow, the idea that there is potential in this thing that could flower and flourish—this is not understood. In order to point up this I want to use two quotations. One is about the beginning of marriage, and one is about the end. Together, I hope they will get over my point.

The one about the beginning is a poem by Jan Struther. It is to two young people who are starting out in marriage. The poet reminds them that they have the raw materials from which a marriage can be built but then points out that raw materials alone do not make art. Having a chisel does not necessarily make one a sculptor, or a pen, a poet. Love, likewise, requires care, judgment, work:

> By patient toil and judgment exquisite
> Of body, mind and heart,
> You may, my innocents, fashion
> This tenderness, this liking, and this passion
> Into a work of art.

And here, from Felix Adler,[1] is a picture of the later years of a good marriage.

Together they have traveled the road of life, and remembrance now holds them close, remembrance of many hours of ineffable felicity, of a sense of union as near to bliss as mortal hearts can realize, of high aspirations pursued in common, of sorrows shared— sacramental sorrows. And now, nearing the end, hand in hand, they look forth upon the wide universe, and the love which they found in themselves and still find there to the last, becomes to them the pledge of a vaster love that moves *beyond* the stars and suns.

---

[1] *Incompatibility in Marriage* (New York: D. Appleton & Co., 1930), p. 15.

7

The
Fruition of Family Life:
Parenthood

The Bible indicates very clearly at the very beginning
that the family is intended to be fruitful. But the biblical view
of parenthood is quite complex; more complex than some
people realize. There are some rather difficult tasks involved in
putting into effect the essential teaching of the Bible about
parenthood in our very different day and generation. We are in
the twentieth century. It is about some of these things that I
want to talk. I realize from the past that you can attempt too
much, and in this chapter I want to focus a little more
narrowly on one or two issues. We just can't cover everything.

For the Hebrews, parenthood was absolutely essential. For
them the concept of procreation was literally "pro-creation."
The Bible properly begins with the divine act of God in
bringing order, being, and life out of nothingness. The Hebrews
were fascinated and moved, as all religious people have been
ever since, by the mystery of the creation of life. For them,
however, the really great thing that God had done was to give to
man the power to continue the work of creation. God had made
living beings at first in his own image; then he had delegated
this power to make living beings in the divine image to man,
and the Hebrews were very deeply aware of this privilege and
this responsibility.

I believe it was not accidental that initiation into the Hebrew
religion was by the rite of circumcision. I think the Hebrews

regarded the penis, the male sex organ, as the most sacred part of their bodies. This was the part of their bodies which they could use to fulfil the supreme spiritual purpose that had been committed to them—the miracle of the creation of new life. And I think that the rite of circumcision was a symbolic rite. It meant the removal of the foreskin as token of the sacrifice of part of the organ in order to symbolize the dedication of all of it. This concept of the sacrifice of part as a symbol of the dedication of the whole is a very widespread religious concept. We have it in tithing. We give a part of our worldly wealth directly to the church. But that doesn't mean that we keep the rest for ourselves. It is a symbol that we dedicate it all. Therefore, I think that circumcision was a very vital part of the Hebrew religion, because it symbolized their very deeply spiritual view of sex and procreation.

It was important in Hebrew times that a man have children, and particularly that he have sons, because his very immortality was wrapped up in this. As you know, the early Hebrews had a very vague concept of immortality as compared with the developed Christian view. They thought of "the fathers," as they called those who had passed on, as living in a kind of shadowy limbo. Their only fulfilment was to look down, as it were, and watch the ongoing activities of those who had followed in their footsteps. They took a brooding interest in the continuation of the family line, and for a Hebrew man to have his line and his name cut off was the final loss of his ongoing identity.

This kind of psychology is somewhat different from ours, but it is very clear and plain in the Old Testament that this was the way the Hebrews felt about themselves. They were preoccupied with the family line. So the most important thing that a man had to do was to beget sons in order that he might give his name, his line, his continuing identity to the future. Therefore, parenthood was absolutely vital for him.

And where did the woman come into the picture? She was, I fear, in a very different category. I don't think we can really understand this until we grasp the rather different view of reproduction and gestation that was widespread in the ancient world. It is a matter of great interest to me that so few people have grasped this significant fact. Perhaps you have to read widely in other cultures in order to understand it.

The essential point is that the ancients had no knowledge of the sperm and the ovum as we have. These scientific facts have only come to light with the invention of the microscope. Before that, people's thoughts of procreation and reproduction were simply based on what they observed. And what seemed logical was that it was the seminal fluid of the male that developed into the child. You can find some passages that suggest this. There is a passage in the book of Job that describes the coagulation of the seminal fluid and the growth into the child. I have found the same concept in ancient Egyptian documents, in ancient Greek documents, and in ancient Hindu documents. It is a widespread belief.

So the Hebrew view of reproduction was that the man, through the male organ dedicated to God through circumcision, deposited the seminal fluid within the body of the woman (they believed within the womb, though we know now that the seminal fluid does not enter the womb) , and that it was there received and nurtured and grew into a child. In some cultures, particularly among some Africans even today, the view was that the menstrual blood of the woman mingled with the male semen and gave it substance, but still it was essentially the seminal fluid of the male that grew into the child.

The implication of this which is significant is that the woman did not contribute anything of her essential self to the child. She nourished it, but that was all. She was the incubator in which the man's child developed, but she was only the instrument—the nurturing instrument. Nothing of herself went into the making of that child. Of course, we now know that the union of sperm and ovum produces a unified new being gathering up in equal measure the chromosomes and genes of the father and of the mother.

But this idea was not understood at all in the ancient world.

You can find this over and over again in the phraseology that was used—the woman is described as the field in which the seed is sown. The male semen is the seed, and you get this idea of the seed in all the ancient cultures. The idea always was that the seed was sown in the earth, and it drew nourishment from the earth, and it sprouted into the flower. But the seed was the seed and the earth was the earth, and they were different. And so the woman was the field in which the seed of the man came to fruition.

This different view from our own explains, I think, a great many things in the Old Testament that are otherwise very hard to understand. It explains, for instance, a good deal of the polygamy that was permitted. There are two kinds of polygamy in the Old Testament. One kind that was never accepted, because it was always thought to be alien to the life of Israel, was the polygamy in which some of the judges and kings, in order to make themselves seem important, followed the patterns of other potentates in the surrounding communities and gathered to themselves vast numbers of wives and concubines as a status symbol of their importance. But the other kind of polygamy *was* accepted under the stern necessity of the situation. For where a man did not have a child by his wife, he was in a sad predicament. His line was not going to be continued. Therefore, although it went against the concept of monogamous marriage, the sheer necessity of the situation permitted him to take another wife in the hope that with her he might have a child—in the hope that she might prove to be a more serviceable receptacle for the growth of his child from his seminal fluid. This was the only acceptable justification for polygamy. It was an extreme measure to meet the exigencies of an extreme situation.

We can see also the meaning of that curious custom of the levirate, by which a man was expected to take to wife the widow of his deceased brother who had no issue. Here was the predicament of a man who had died without issue. His line was cut off, and as a desperate measure to save the situation it was permissible for his brother or his next of kin, who had the same seed as he had, to use his wife to raise up seed to the name of the dead brother. So, even beyond the eleventh hour, the immortality of the dead brother might yet be redeemed, his line continued through a child who could carry on his name, born at least of his wife if not of himself.

This concept of gestation explains also, in a more satisfying way than any other that I have found, the double standard of sex morality that we find in the Old Testament, and that we find running all through the patriarchal family in all human cultures. Remember that there was no concept of illegitimacy in the Old Testament. There could not be. A man's children were all his own, wherever they were nurtured; whether they were nurtured in the womb of his legal wife or in that of a concubine or even of a prostitute. They were all his children, because they were all grown from his seed—the seed of his body. And, therefore, it was never considered wrong for a man to commit adultery against his wife. This was not a conceivable idea to the Hebrews. A man was sexually free, and we even find some quite important people in Israel having sex relations with prostitutes. In Genesis 38 you will find the story of one of them. Prostitution is, of course, considered unwise and rather undesirable, but there is never a sense of deep moral wrong about it unless the man has sex relations with a *religious* prostitute.

There are two kinds of prostitutes in the Bible. If a Hebrew man has sex relations with a religious prostitute this is an awful act of apostasy, because he has used the very organ dedicated to God in an activity that is involved in fertility rites to another god. This is apostasy of the deepest kind. But apart from this, for a man in Hebrew society to have sex relations with another woman was never taken very seriously.

On the other hand, for a married woman to have sex relations with another man was atrocious. This was the last betrayal of her trust, because if a man could not be sure that the child that grew within the body of his wife was his child, then he might be deceived in the darkest way. The woman who committed adultery against her husband by having sex relations with another man falsified her husband's line. She failed in her deepest responsibility. Therefore, there was a very strict standard of chastity and fidelity imposed upon the woman, but no corresponding standard imposed upon the man. But this was not as is commonly supposed because the woman was regarded as inferior. It was because the woman's function reproductively was essentially different, and her integrity was vitally important, while the man's integrity didn't matter very much. Out of these ideas and other ideas there grew up the double standard of morality that has run right through all the great human cultures and continued in our Western culture until today.

There is just one idea that I want to add to this rather sketchy picture of parenthood in the Bible. Normally a man found that his wife bore him children. But when occasionally she didn't, people were puzzled why it should be so. If the man had well and truly deposited the seminal fluid in the body of the woman, why didn't she have a child? The obvious explanation to these simple Hebrews was that God had closed the womb of the woman. The door had been closed; therefore, she had not received the seminal fluid to nurture it until it grew into a child. This was regarded as a mark of the divine disfavor. So throughout the Old Testament we find barrenness regarded as a curse that has fallen upon the childless woman. This is also found in all the great patriarchal cultures. If you have ever been to India and visited some of the Hindu temples, you have no doubt seen the agony and the dereliction of the childless women as they come to pray that God will open their wombs. All through the ages, women in patriarchal cultures have suffered in this way.

In the Bible, therefore, parenthood is regarded as a glorious and blessed fulfilment. It is the fulfilment of the essential purpose for which a man exists. It is the fulfilment of the essential purpose for which a woman exists. It is a mark of God's blessing, and the coming of a child is an occasion of great, deep, and lasting happiness.

Despite that fact, oddly enough, if you take the trouble to go through the Bible and count them up, you will find that there were very few large families in the Bible. Most families are relatively small. This has puzzled me a great deal, and the only conclusion I can come to is based on the known fact that the Hebrew women suckled their children for quite long periods of time, even for years. Now we do know that, at least among primitive women, continued nursing tends to produce temporary sterility. This may be one of the explanations, although there may well be others, why the Bible doesn't report very large families.

It is a long way to jump, from that old picture of a rather simple, devout awareness of God's continuous working in procreation and a wholly positive acceptance of sex as God's almost greatest gift to man, to our confused modern world. The great distinctive factor in our modern world is that now we have planned parenthood. I don't know whether you saw a recent story in the *Reader's Digest* about the family in Connecticut, where there has been a lot of talk about planned parenthood. The parents were talking about this, and the boy suddenly chipped in and said, "Oh, I think planned parenthood is a very good idea. I can think of several things about my parents that could be better planned."

Whether we like it or not, planned parenthood has changed much of our thinking today. Now it is *we* who open and close the womb, and this is a very profound and searching responsibility. There are some religious people who for that reason do not believe in planned parenthood. The Catholic Church, as you know, has taken a strong attitude about this, and other religious people are confused about it. We are all entitled to our own ideas, but we had better realize that planned parenthood is with us to stay. There is no going back. So we have to try to make sense of it as best we can.

The churches at first tended to be very opposed to planned parenthood, but there has been a marked change of attitude in recent years, particularly with the development of the theological concept of the unitive end in marriage alongside the procreative end. We talked about that previously. Sherwin

Bailey, whose writings I have referred to, has given us a new concept of the enormous importance of the unitive end of marriage. His view is that, in order to preserve the unitive end, control of the procreative end under the guidance of God is right and good. This is the attitude that is being taken now by a great many Christians after much thought and study and prayer.

In many other fields, power that we formerly did not have is now in our hands—power that we can use to the glory of God or abuse to our own destruction. It does not seem to me that the possession of this power in itself can be wrong. Somebody once said that science is thinking God's thoughts after him—a rather good definition of science, I think. Science is not creating anything that isn't already there. Science is only gaining a deeper understanding of the wonder and the marvel of the universe that God has made for us. And surely God means for us to develop that understanding. If, therefore, more power and more control come into our hands, perhaps this means that as God's children we are growing up, just as our own children gain more power and more control, make decisions and accept moral responsibility, as *they* grow up.

Of course, there is no escaping the moral responsibility that goes with birth control. Those who believe in planned parenthood (and some of the most devout Christian people do) are aware that this puts into man's hands a tremendous responsibility. To describe our situation, some of our theological thinkers use the phrase "responsible Christian parenthood." If we ourselves now have the power to open and close the womb, then surely we must diligently seek the will of God as to when we exercise that power.

This puts us in a situation in which we have hardly ever been before—a situation in which we have to examine our *motives* for parenthood. It is astonishing how few people have ever thought of motives for parenthood. But I think this is an important question, and I want to say a word or two about it. In the old days, it was a simple matter. People said, "However many children come—if it is none, or one, or a dozen—we accept this as the will of God. We just have sex relations in marriage and accept the issue, whatever it is." This sounds very beautiful and very simple. But if we feel that *we* have some responsibility in this matter, as most of us do, then we have to ask ourselves not only *when* we exercise that responsibility, but *why* we exercise that responsibility. What are our motives in wanting to have children?

For the ancient Hebrew, the main motive was that he must continue his family line. He must build up Israel in the years to come. To some extent we also have that motive. But, in fact, there are many motives for seeking to have children. There is for example the motive of self-preservation, the idea that you want to project yourself into the future, to produce a sort of further addition of yourself. This is curiously manifested in American culture (though oddly enough not in British culture) by the concept of John Smith, Jr. and John Smith III. The idea is that to a certain extent John Smith is going to live on again and have another life in his son who carries the same name, and in a sense carries the same identity.

Up to a point this is a noble concept, but it has some quite grave dangers. If you think of your child as a projection of yourself, you may in your raising of your child deny him his own identity. We have all seen situations in which parents have been unconsciously trying to live out in their own children the life that they were unable to live themselves, trying to get their children to achieve what they didn't achieve, trying to make their children dramatizations in another generation of their own ideal selves, and forgetting that their children require the respect due to individuals in their own right.

Another motivation for parenthood is that a woman has maternal urges that she wants to fulfil—the aching arms of the woman who wants to embrace a child. The aching arms are all right, and the urge for maternity is certainly a God-given urge; but is it a sufficient reason to have children, in order that those children may satisfy physiological and psychological need in yourself? Is it a sound idea to have children, as some people do, to shore up a shaky marriage? No, I don't think so. You cannot expect a child to meet your needs, to save your marriage. A child lives his own life. He goes out into his own world. So you see in those ways we can invest ourselves in our children to their own detriment.

Another motivation for parenthood is that children will look after us later in life. When my first daughter was born I remember a friend commiserating with me because I had a daughter. By way of consolation, she added, "Never mind, she'll take care of you in your old age!" Perhaps we have rather lost that hope nowadays, but in the past it *has* been a motivation for parenthood.

Another motivation for parenthood is just keeping up with the Joneses. A young couple becomes aware that all the other people on the street have a baby in a buggy and they don't, so they get desperate about it. The child can be a status symbol, and I believe that one of our problems in the United States today is that the child has become a status symbol because we have run out of other status symbols. It is no longer exceptional to have a big car with fins, or a little car without fins, or a split-level house; and I have seen cases of parents who are looking to their cute or successful children to be status symbols for them, to make them feel that they are at least as good as the Joneses, and maybe a little bit better.

These are doubtful motivations for parenthood, and we may well ask ourselves in the face of all this what are the true Christian motivations for parenthood? There must be many, but I want to mention only two. The first is that the nature of love is creative. Therefore, people who are truly in love and who have found deep love in each other will want to bestow that love, to give it in sharing and in service and in caring. It is true that when a man and woman first fall in love, their love involves them in deep preoccupation with one another. We think of young lovers as gazing adoringly into each other's eyes. But that sort of love isn't going to last. Two people who gaze adoringly into each other's eyes long enough will develop a squint!

So the time will come when they must turn away from one another and stand side by side looking outward toward the task that they have to do and the ministry that they have to accomplish. Parenthood is one significant experience that takes them away from their preoccupation with themselves and unites them in a projection of the overflow of their love upon the child, who needs above all else an abundance of love. So the creativeness of love is a deep and true Christian motive for having children.

The other motive I am going to mention is our faith in the future, our faith in God's purpose. I have heard married couples during the war years, and particularly during the bombing of London, say, "We are not going to bring children into this kind of world." This shows a lack of faith in the future and in God's purpose. We have children because we believe that the things we stand for, the things we care about, are going on to fruition. We have that faith, and we want our children to take up the torch where we left it and carry it on into the future.

Some years ago I coined a definition of parenthood, and it aroused a good deal of interest. Here it is. "Parenthood is the payment we make to the future for the debt we owe to the past." I wanted to stress the fact that as parents we have no vested interest in our children. They are not even ours in the last resort. They are entrusted to us, but they are not our possessions. All the service that we give to them is simply a return, a grateful, glad return for the service which we ourselves received in our helpless and tender years from our parents and from the others who loved us and cared for us.

Rabindranath Tagore, the Indian poet, has said something very beautiful about this. He said, "God sends every little child into the world with the message that he has not yet despaired of man." And having children is, therefore, a supreme act of faith in God, and in his continuing purpose in the future.

Now I want to talk about something different. I have given a lot of attention to motivation for parenthood, because this is a neglected subject, and I think it is a crucial issue in our Christian thinking. But I don't want to forget that when the children come, they still have to be brought up! They need raising and they need training, too. And here we encounter the second major challenge as Christians in thinking through the meaning of Christian parenthood today: How do we train children in a free society?

The biblical concept of bringing up children was based on the idea of shaping and molding plastic clay—even hammering it into shape, because according to the old familiar adage, "Spare the rod and you will spoil the child." So the idea was that you beat and hammer the personality of the child—the plastic clay—into the shape you want him to be.

This concept of parenthood has continued almost into our own time. For instance, here is something that Susanna Wesley,[1] the mother of the founder of the Methodist Church, who brought up a great many children, said about the subject.

In order to form the minds of children, the first thing to be done is to conquer their will and bring them to an obedient temper. To inform the understanding is a work of time, and must with children proceed by slow degrees, as they are able to bear it; but the subjecting the will is a thing that must be done at once, and the sooner the better.

That doesn't quite agree with the sort of things that we are reading in our books on child care and child development today, does it?

How do we reconcile those very different concepts? The answer I think lies in an elaboration of the point that I was making before. Whether we like it or not, we are living in an era in which the freedom of the individual to flower in responsible choice and autonomy is the basic principle. I do not think of this as an unchristian principle. I think it is based fundamentally on the unlimited worth of the individual. But it

---

[1] Eliza Clark, *Susanna Wesley* ("Eminent Women Series," ed. John H. Ingram [London: W. H. Allen & Co., 1886]) , p. 31.

does mean that bringing up children today requires a new kind of approach.

We are no longer bringing up our children in a patriarchal culture, to take their appointed place within the culture and stay there. This was the old concept, and it still is the concept if you go to the East today. My wife and I dealt with this rather fully in our book, *Marriage: East and West,* where we described the Oriental idea that every person has a proper place in a tightly constructed society, and he must learn to accept that place and never question it. There is no getting ahead. There's no room for development. You don't have ambitions. You accept your lot in patient, obedient resignation.

If you are bringing up children in order that they may fit into that kind of culture, of course you must break their will and teach them obedience. Otherwise, they will be restless rebels all their lives. But if you are bringing up children to live in a democratic society, with almost unlimited freedom and choice, with the unlimited right to move up and down the social scale and do all the things that other people are doing in our culture, if you train them to be obedient and resigned, you will make them incapable of functioning in that sort of society, because nobody is going to give them orders. This is the great problem in the Christian raising of children today.

We cannot deny them freedom. Therefore, we have no course but to teach them to use freedom responsibly according to the will of God. This is really another aspect of what we have already been talking about—the freedom to choose to have children or not to have children, to open and to close the womb.

We carry much greater moral responsibility in this kind of society than people did in the ancient world. Consequently, working out a pattern for the Christian raising of children is very difficult. Indeed, I feel a great deal of sympathy for the man who said he started with seven theories and no children and ended with seven children and no theories!

But Christians must grapple with this. There is no doubt that in our current society we see plenty of evidences of freedom run riot—freedom that has gone too far, freedom that has been accorded to young people before they are ready for it and before they can exercise it responsibly. We see this in the patterns of early dating and the inevitable sexual experiences that it leads to. Never before has there been a human culture in which immature young people have been allowed to be alone together late at night in cars. In our Western tradition, as well as in the great Eastern cultures, young girls have always been protected against the predatory male and against their own sex impulses. If we give up protecting our girls, we impose upon them in these early years a degree of freedom that they are simply not able to handle. And when these girls get in trouble and become pregnant it isn't their fault. We must not blame them; we must not judge them. We have exposed them to influences that they were unable to handle.

That is one illustration among others of the abuse of freedom. There is plenty abuse of freedom in our American society. We run up the flag of freedom, and we bow before it. But the one thing we never do is to take it down and examine it and study it. If we did we would realize that freedom is a horror unless it is exercised with mature responsibility.

What is the answer? The best way I can approach this is to consider what it is that a child needs from his parents, particularly in our modern world and in terms of Christian parenthood. I am going to identify four universal needs of the child and make a few brief comments on how Christian parents have to struggle with the meeting of these needs.

1. The first need is *love*. Obviously we have to love our children. But again, we talk about love but we don't stop to examine it. We have to love our children, not in a conditional way, but in an unconditional way, as God loves us. This is the meaning of Christian parenthood in terms of love—that we must try to love our children as God loves us. That is not easy. Our children are difficult and awkward, as we are difficult and awkward. Henry Drummond once said that God's love for poor

sinners is very wonderful, but God's patience with ill-natured saints is a deeper mystery! Sometimes we are ill-natured saints, and as God bears with us at those times, so we must bear with our children. We cannot say to our children, "If you do what displeases me, I will withdraw my love, I will reject you." We cannot do that as Christian parents. God's love goes to the limit for us, and our love must go to the limit for our children.

This doesn't mean that we should indulge our children. I'll have something to say about that later. It doesn't mean we don't discipline them; but it means that our children know that whatever they do, however they vex us, however they let us down, we will never stop loving them. This seems to me to be a fundamental principle of Christian parenthood. I wish I could share with you a little poem by Coventry Patmore, of which I am very fond. As a father he lost his temper, and he spanked his child and sent him up to bed. He was a widower. Then afterwards his conscience troubled him, and he stood before his sleeping child and thought of how harsh he had been; then he remembered God's patience with him. Through that experience of disciplining his child thoughtlessly and withdrawing his love he found a deepened awareness of God's patience with him, and he saw how his parenthood was really a challenge to express and live out his realization of the way God was dealing with him.

2. Second, *discipline*. Our children need discipline. Not ought to have it, but *need* it. If you deny a child discipline you take from him something essential for his growth. You don't do him a service by letting him do what he likes.

In the old days, the main purpose of discipline was to lick the child into shape, to break his will and make him obedient. This is not the goal of discipline today. If we do that, we make children unfit to live in the world of freedom. If you have only been taught obedience, how can you accept moral responsibility in a free world?

Today, the one purpose of discipline is to establish clearly and plainly in the experience of the child that this is a world of law and order, even if it doesn't look like it. This means that discipline must be consistent. You fail terribly in discipline if parents don't share the same principles and stand by one another and create a consistent world for the child so that he knows that this is wrong, not today, not yesterday, not tomorrow, but always. Thus he has a clear sense of values. It is through discipline that we give him values.

At the same time, through discipline the child learns self-discipline. A great purpose of discipline is to teach the child to discipline himself, and as soon as possible. We support him with discipline until he can build his own supports around him. Our children today are going to live in a world of widely conflicting values, where they will have to make moral choices all the time. If they do not have self-discipline, heaven help them.

3. Third, a child needs *support* and *protection*. An English writer makes a rather wonderful comparison between the development of the child in the womb before birth and the development of the child in the family after birth. He says that the family is the cultural womb of the child. Just as the child was taking shape out of the elements in the dark, enclosed protection of the womb, until his body was well enough and strong enough to go out into the world, so the child's personality is protected and enclosed in the womb of the family until it has grown sufficiently for him to be able to go out as an independent being and live his own life. The family provides him with that necessary supportive framework.

We have talked previously about the way in which people who come from good families, where there's a good family fellowship and a warm sense of support, are always better equipped for marriage and, indeed, better equipped for life as a whole. Many of the young people who get into trouble do so because they do not feel warm emotional support in their home. They are deeply estranged from their parents, and they may rush into early marriage to try to find the sense of emotional warmth and support that they are lacking.

4. Fourth, the child needs to have *respect* shown for his de-

veloping individuality and the right to move toward *independence*. This is the supreme task that the home must fulfil—to prepare the child to stand on his own feet as an independent adult. Somebody once said that the whole art of parenthood is summed up in five words: "Love 'em and leave 'em." Love them yes, but don't impose your love upon them. Don't smother them with love, don't make unreasonable demands of them. But give them freedom to grow, freedom to find themselves, freedom to be themselves. You cannot make over your child, your child must live his own life. As Kahlil Gibran,[2] the Lebanese poet, said:

> You may give them your love but not your thoughts.
> For they have their own thoughts.
> You may house their bodies but not their souls,
> For their souls dwell in the house of tomorrow.

Some of you may be saying, "Why has he said nothing about the Christian training of the child?" Actually, I have been saying nothing else! This is what I have been talking about all the time! Of course we must communicate with our children; of course we must tell them what we believe; of course we must share with them the great experiences of our faith. But it is not our words that do this. It is the spirit of the home that does it. And if our words are belied by our deeds, then our words are empty and thin. As Emerson once said, "I can't hear what you say, because what you are is shouting at me." This might be the response of many children who hear the words but do not feel the spirit.

It is in the way we live in our homes with our children, in the way we love them, the way we support them, the way we respect them, the way we care for them, that we are teaching them Christian truth moment by moment. I once said some years ago something else about parenthood: I solemnly believe that parenthood is the most Godlike act of which man is capable. There is no experience in life that tests us more than parenthood. It searches us, it humbles us, it makes us aware of our deep

---

[2] *The Prophet* (New York: Alfred A. Knopf, 1957), p. 18. Used by permission.

shortcomings, because it is the most Godlike act of which we are capable. It is here if anywhere that we have to try, weak and feeble as we are, to be sufficiently like God for our children perhaps to catch in us and in our ways and in our love and in our caring a glimpse of what the Heavenly Father is truly like.

8

The Family
in Its Social Environment

Plato once said, "The state is the family writ large." The state, that is to say, is simply an extension of the family. But that is no longer true in our modern world. Our great complex nation-states are not extensions of families; they are rather vast agglomerations of families. And in the interaction between family and society there can be a great deal of conflict. It is the family that prepares the future citizens of the society, and it is the society that sets the requirements and standards for future citizens. So in any society that is in a state of equilibrium, the family and the society must have the same goals; they must be working to produce the same kinds of persons, to function in the same kinds of ways. I think it can be said with truth that if the family, and the society to which it belongs, are in conflict with one another, a battle will have to be fought out in which sooner or later either the society changes the family or the family changes the society.

We see a very good illustration of this kind of struggle in what has been happening in the Soviet Union for nearly fifty years. My wife and I have just completed a very extensive study of the Soviet family, and we have seen how the Communists broke up the old Russian patriarchal family and then tried to mold the family to be the instrument of their will. But the family clung to some of its values, and those values finally had to be accepted by the state. After a long period of struggle, a condition of equilibrium was arrived at, which now may be found in the Soviet Union.

So the family and the society must sooner or later come to terms if there is to be a healthy, stable community. Our American family, in the early pioneer days, was very like the Bible family in many respects. It was patriarchal. Here is an interesting description from Hornell and Ella Hart's book, *Personality and the Family,*[1] of the functions which the early American family discharged:

> The home was the factory during the first two centuries after our ancestors began to settle America. Industries pursued in many households included churning, canning, pickling, drying fruits and vegetables, butchering, making sausage and lard, smoking and salting meat, making candles, soap and medicine, producing maple sugar and honey, baking and cooking all food consumed, repairing shoes and harness, spinning, sewing, knitting and tailoring the family clothing, laundering all clothing and linen by hand, repairing wagons, carriages, and tools, providing the family water supply and disposing of sewage, building and repairing houses, furniture, barns and sheds.

If you had followed this with a check list, how many would you have found that your family is now carrying out? You see, the family was very self-contained. In addition, the members of the family, almost all of them, worked together on the homestead. A great deal of the education and guidance of the children in social values was provided in the home. Recreation was provided almost entirely in the home or in the homes of a group of neighbors. The social life of the family went on around the homesteads of a particular group of friends and neighbors, so that families were the center of the throbbing life of the community.

Today the family has changed radically in this respect. It has lost the great majority of the functions that it discharged for its members, and in so far as any of these are left, gadgets now perform them for us. I was talking recently with some indi-

---

[1] (Boston: D. C. Heath & Co., 1935).

viduals about engaging the members of the family in the creative life of the home. One man said he had a boy of nine. He went on to explain that when he was a boy of that age, he used to fetch the coal, deal with the furnace, and do endless other things in and around the house. But he said, "Now there isn't a thing for this boy of mine to do, except feed the dog and take the garbage outside to the can. And already they have a machine that will destroy the garbage so we don't have to put it into the can."

Our life has become so mechanized, so laborsaving as a result of these tremendous technological advances, and we are assured that there are plenty more to come. Did you know that 90 per cent of all the scientists who have ever lived in the history of the world are alive and working today? What they will come up with in the next fifty years baffles the imagination. Already we buy in the stores all the things that the family used to make, for cash. Therefore, we have to have plenty of cash. In order to earn the cash to buy the gadgets and other things at the stores, we have to go out to work; and sometimes not only father spends most of his time away from the home community, but mother also is out at work all day.

The family no longer provides its own recreation. I can remember when we first came over from England, thirteen and a half years ago, and settled in an American community, our children were invited to parties. We had had many parties at home. But when they went out to American parties they discovered that the parents of their friends had no ideas about running a party in the old style. They just had the kids look at television, or they hired a cart and took them on a hayride, or they drove them all in to New York to a circus.

At our parties at home in England we had a program of games and competitions that went riotously on for hour after hour. But the art of making home recreation has very largely gone, and now our homes are invaded by machines that pour out to us in tabloid form the mass entertainment that is cooked up for us. The outside world with all its confused and mingled values penetrates our living rooms, our dining nooks, and even our bedrooms.

Similarly, our social life has shifted very largely away from the home and from the family as a participating unit. The social life of American communities is often very fragmented; the man goes to his particular recreational group, the woman goes to her group, the senior highs to their group, and junior highs to theirs, and so on all down the line. The family goes in all directions, and there is not much left that the whole family can do together. Indeed, for many people in our culture today the home is not much more than a place where you go to eat and sleep.

Not only is it true that the home has been shorn of many of its functions; it has also, again and again, been deprived of its rootage. We live in an era of tremendous social mobility. One family in five, we are told, moves to a new home every year. When you break down this figure into realistic terms, as somebody once did, it means that every day in the United States twenty-five thousand families, representing about a tenth of a million people, are on the road with all their worldly goods, moving from one home to another.

In this great melting pot, in which families are cast together, there is a constant process of mixing, of leveling down, which deprives many families of their uniqueness, of their identity, and moves them into a common mold. We have seen over and over again, in our studies of immigrant families, how these families, coming from other cultures and settling in the United States, strive to hold on to the traditions in which they were raised, and may succeed in the first generation. But inevitably in the second generation, as the children go out into the community and to the schools, the old values break down, and by the third generation they are almost totally effaced, and these people are merged in the great American mass. This, of course, has its value. It brings unity and solidarity to the community. But this is achieved at the cost of the gradual scaling down and loss of identity that goes on all the time.

When the family has been shorn of so many of its functions, the focus of family life shifts to the meeting of needs of an essentially emotional nature. The need for emotional security becomes acute in a bewildering, very impersonal world, where everything is shifting and you don't know what you can be sure about. The need for affection becomes acute in a world where you often feel you have been reduced, in terms of identity, to little more than a Social Security number. There is the need that somebody should know you as a unique individual, accept you for what you are, and love you for what you are. There is the need for intimacy in the constant moving among great crowds. There is the need to get closer to somebody in some sort of more real relationship.

It is said that in the Middle Ages in Europe many, many people—perhaps the majority of the people—went from the cradle to the grave and never saw more than one hundred other human faces. When you think of the vast multitudes with which we are mingled and lost in our great cities today, we crave for a sense of personal significance and identity and worth. We bring these needs, sharpened and accentuated, to the home in the hope that there they may be met.

However, when we consider the family in our American culture today, and the pressures of the culture on the family, we must recognize that not all of these pressures are harmful. I want to stress this. Of necessity I am talking here about some of the unfavorable ones, because they create so many of our problems. But I want to say, very clearly and definitely, that there are some very fine values in American culture that are supportive of the family. The homes that we have are the finest in the world. Our standards of health, and the way our health is safeguarded, are wonderful. Our standards of living make us all like princes in a world which, beyond our shores, is peopled with many very underprivileged people. For all this we should be grateful.

But there are in this society of ours some very distorted values, and this is what the Christian families of our times have to face. So I must place some emphasis upon these weaker elements of

American culture. There are values that are distorted, that are insidious, that are destructive of all that is best in our Christian way of life.

I want to emphasize three of these false values which I think are very characteristic of our culture at the present time. First, there is a false emphasis on wealth. Second, there is a false emphasis on status. Third, there is a false emphasis on sex. I want to speak of these false emphases, of what they are doing, and of what they can do if we let them infiltrate into our families.

1. First, the false emphasis on *wealth*. We are living, we are told, in an affluent society. The per capita income in the United States, the last time I saw the figures, was nearing $3,000. The per capita income in some adjoining Caribbean countries, like Jamaica and Trinidad, is little more than $200. The per capita income in India is $70. The per capita income in Pakistan, and in Haiti, is $60. These figures will demonstrate how wealthy we are. In fact, American families today have so much money that they don't really need, that enormous industries are working at full pressure to relieve them of their surplus cash in exchange for articles that don't do them much good and sometimes do them a great deal of harm.

The result of this prodigal practice is that in North America, according to Margaret Mead, 7 per cent of the world's population is consuming about 50 per cent of the world's natural resources. And yet, when ratings are made of family problems in the United States, financial problems nearly always head the list! This is true in spite of the fact that, compared with most other peoples in the world today, and compared with our own forefathers, we are very, very rich.

Of course, there's nothing basically wrong with money as such. It is just a convenient means of exchange. Yet money can be a grave peril, as Jesus reminded us. Wealth can lead us into all kinds of dangerous traps. Money can distort our values until money becomes an end in itself. The quest for money can also turn life into competition instead of co-operation. Look at the mad rush of our suburban families to keep up with the Joneses. Money can become a means of exploitation. Charge what the traffic will bear, we say; when what we *ought* to say is, charge what the product is worth.

Money can make us soft and luxury-loving, till the body rules the spirit, and bound by the silken chains of self-indulgence we become the helpless prisoners of our extravagant habits. Then we try to escape by cheating nature. For instance, millions of Americans today are looking hopefully for a pill that will enable them to overeat without suffering the natural consequences of overeating!

2. Second, there is in our culture a false emphasis on *status*. Vance Packard has reminded us that we are a nation of status seekers. We are desperate for recognition. We talk about keeping up with the Joneses. However, a recent article in the *New York Times* said that the real trouble is that we are not content to *keep up with* the Joneses; we want to *get ahead* of the Joneses!

Why all this tremendous emphasis on status? I think it is because the simple rural community life has broken down, and our security has gone with it. More and more we are crowding together in great urban masses. Sometimes when I go into New York City and see more and more of these skyscrapers going up on Manhattan Island, I say, "What extraordinary people we are! Here we have a vast, beautiful country in which to live; yet millions and millions of us are packing ourselves tighter and tighter together on this one tiny little island!"

This is not only happening in Manhattan. Everywhere there is a tremendous flow to the great cities. The trouble about the great cities is that in them you feel a very small person in a very big crowd, and you realize that you have to shout loud to draw attention to yourself or nobody may notice you at all.

A recent book that I read contains a very searching indictment of this quest for exaggerated status in American society. It is Daniel Boorstin's book, *The Image*.[2] He says that we have lost

---

[2] (New York: Atheneum, 1962) , pp. 45, 57–58.

our heroes, we have lost our sense of the great men we honored in the past. Nowadays, instead, we worship celebrities, and here I quote:

> One of the oldest of man's visions was the flash of divinity in the great man. . . . The secret of his greatness was God's secret. His generation thanked God for him. . . . Two centuries ago when a great man appeared, people looked for God's purpose in him; today we look for his press agent. . . . Our age has produced a new kind of eminence. . . . This new kind of eminence is "celebrity.". . . *The celebrity is a person who is known for his well-knownness.* . . . He is neither good nor bad, great nor petty. . . . He is made by all of us who willingly read about him, who like to see him on television, who buy recordings of his voice.

This quest for status touches all of us.

3. Third, there is in our culture a false emphasis on *sex*. I wonder if we all realize how much American culture, compared with most other cultures in the world today, is sex saturated. Today sex almost dominates our social customs, our literature, our entertainment, and our advertising. By contrast, in the Soviet Union you will find little or no erotic material in books or magazines, in movies or theater plays, on radio or TV. But on returning to the United States, you are met by a wave of sexual stimulation on the newsstands, everywhere in the advertising world, and throughout the entertainment media, which brings home to you, as somebody put it, the fact that in this country we are never allowed to forget for long that God created us male and female!

I am not suggesting that there's anything wrong with sex as such. What bothers me is not the emphasis on sex but the distortion of sex. It is all right for a woman to make herself sexually attractive to her husband; but need she also make herself sexually attractive to every other man she meets? Isn't that needlessly complicating the issue? It is all right to say that sex is a part of life, and it may be all right to say that sex should be portrayed as a part of life in our literature and in our movies; but when our movies have to feed us more and more sexual pathology in order to titillate our jaded senses, haven't we gotten this thing out of perspective?

I was in a southern town recently. I arrived on Saturday evening, and in my hotel room I found a copy of the evening paper, which I probably wouldn't have bought otherwise. I looked at it, and on the whole of the back page there was an advertisement of the movies. I made a careful extract of the contents of this page. The heading said, "Movies Are Your Best Entertainment." The page contained thirteen pictures of women partially undressed, and one apparently totally undressed. Here are some of the captions: (1) "Here she is in all her brazen glory, the most notorious woman of an immoral age"; (2) "Half-man, half-beast, he sold his soul for passion"; (3) "Nudists on the high seas"; (4) "Naked innocence"; (5) "Nightmare of horror"; (6) "Inside them raged desires and fears screaming to explode" (a picture of two young people facing one another); (7) "The pure hell of St. Trinian's"; (8) "Sex kittens go to college"; and (9) "Love is my profession," by that unhappy little French girl who a little later attempted to commit suicide.

This was commended as "your best entertainment" in a southern American city. Need I say more about the distortion of sex in our culture? It even gets into our teaching about sex. It is all right to encourage husbands and wives to enjoy their sex relations as an expression of their love; but when you reduce marital sex to a push-button technique that you have to be able to carry out just as the books describe it, or you are a failure, then I think the time has come to throw the books away. Sure, sex is a very important *expression* of the love between husbands and wives, but the trouble is that in our culture today we are trying to make it a *substitute* for love. We are trying to make sex a cure for loneliness, a panacea for insecurity, a remedy for boredom, an energizer, a tranquilizer and an elixir all rolled into one. It cannot be done.

Now I want to look at the way in which these pressures are affecting our families. We are living, as we have seen, in a culture that has some distorted values. What is this doing to us? Let's have a quick rundown of some of the effects of these distorted values on the various members of our families.

1. First, on *children*. There's no doubt at all in my mind as to what the social pressures of our culture are doing to our children. It is making them *grow up fast*.

We have been hearing plenty lately about early dating. Did you see the issue of *Life* in 1962 that showed some of our precocious twelve-year-olds? I was reading recently about one study, somewhere in the South, in which boys and girls of ten who had already started going on dates acknowledged that half of them had been having kissing experiences. The comment was, "If they are kissing at ten, what will they be doing at fifteen?"

What makes them that way? Wherever I go, and whenever I ask a group of intelligent, thoughtful citizens, they always give me the same answer. They say it is the mothers of the girls, wanting their kids to be cute and popular. It has gone so far that I hear someone has written an article called, "Are We Trying to Abolish Childhood?"

At the White House Conference on Children and Youth in 1960, a speaker with great eloquence took as his theme, "Let the Children Be Children." He charged that we are robbing our children of the golden age of childhood—that period in late childhood and early adolescence when they need to be left to themselves, quietly to find the depths of their own nature. Instead of leaving them to themselves, we are pushing them with all sorts of pressures into paired relationships.

I remember one year, here in the United States, I was talking to a PTA meeting. A woman came up to me afterwards and said, "I have a daughter of fifteen, and she doesn't have a boyfriend. What's the matter with her?" A little later that same year, back in England, I spoke to a similar group; and believe it or not, a woman came up to me afterwards and said, "I have a daughter of fifteen, and she's got a boyfriend. What's the matter with her?"

2. What are these pressures doing to our *youth?* Take the girls first. Social pressure on the growing girl I think is quite clear. It is to *get a man.* Get an education, sure; have a good time, of course; but whatever else you do or don't do—get a man and get married. That way, you will prove you are smart, you will prove you are a real woman. That way, you will get every-thing—wealth, status, and sex. This "husband-hunting hys-teria," as I have called it, is a terrible pressure for many of our girls. I have talked with girls of eighteen or nineteen, just out of high school, who are nearly in despair because they are not yet married and don't yet see marriage on the horizon. It makes them anxious; it makes them troubled; it makes them feel they are no good; it sometimes drives them to make themselves cheap in their efforts to hold on to a boy. And often it drives them into premature and disastrous marriages.

And what about the boys? The pressure on them is very definitely to *get ahead.* "All men are created equal," you say here in the United States, and then you add "but get ahead!" Already in their early or middle teens these boys want to act grownup; and often that means tearing around in a fast car, getting drunk, and exploiting the opposite sex. This gives them status in their own group, there's no doubt about it. This is the basis of status. But in order to do this they have to have money, and so you see the vicious circle has started already.

3. What is our culture doing to *young married couples?* The first pressure on them, of course, is *be happily married.* And this is fine within reason, but often it isn't within reason. It is absurd to expect any human relationship to bring perpetual happiness to anybody. Continued happiness would be a most sterile and damaging condition to live in. The nature of human life is struggle, and if we can't accept it that way we can't start really living. To all of us, of course, there come experiences of great and supreme happiness. There come also experiences of great sorrow. Most of life is lived between those two extremes. We can't be happy all the time. This is not the way life is made.

The other pressure on the young married couple is to *keep busy*. If American couples can't find perpetual happiness, they try to make up for it by living in a state of perpetual motion. Everyone who comes to this country notices the mad American tempo, everyone rushing around in a hurry and blowing their horns like mad if they have to wait at the traffic light even for a moment. This tragic pressure can wither, all too often, young marriages. These young couples sometimes have no time to communicate, no time to relax and reflect, no time to keep in love, no time to make their homes a place of peace.

4. What are the pressures on *parents?* Oh, there are so many pressures on the parents. I mention only two of them. The first one is *give your children all the things you didn't have.* In a land of plenty, of course, it is very natural that we should want to heap gifts and opportunities on our children, hoping to keep them happy. But often all we are doing is conditioning them at an early age to false values, giving them a need for wealth and gratification, denying them the struggles and the hardships out of which growing young people build strength and character. And it is worse still when parents try to make their gifts take the place of their own love and comradeship and patience and understanding. "My father gave me everything," said one juvenile delinquent to the judge, "except his time and his real interest and his love."

The other pressure on parents is *be psychologically sophisticated.* You know what I mean by that, don't you? Of course we want parents to be wise, we want them to understand child development, we want them to benefit from all our rich modern treasuries of knowledge. But how we have threatened, warned, castigated, and scared our poor trembling parents into helpless paralysis by presenting them with awful pictures of their children as being as frail and fragile as Dresden china, until they could no longer act like strong self-willed adults any more! No child wants a walking psychology text for a parent. He wants and needs an average human being, not free from faults and weaknesses, but one who accepts his responsibilities, who is

prepared to give love, to go on giving love, and, when the
occasion requires it, prepared to administer discipline firmly
and decisively.

5. What is our culture doing to the *older married couples?*
There is no doubt about the pressure on these older family
members. "Act young" is the message. "Don't give way to your
age! Behave as if you were still in your prime! Cling doggedly
to youth, and never surrender!" Could anything be more
stupid? And yet this is a powerful pressure in American society.
By contrast, think of the way in which the older cultures honor
age and allow old people to be old. Here, the aging woman
worries to death over her gray hair and her wrinkled face, while
the man throws a fit if he feels his sexual potency is beginning to
slip.

Look at some of the insurance ads that you see. "How I
retired in fifteen years with $300 a month." And the people in
the pictures look so youthful and vigorous that I mistake them
for my graduate students! Here is an account of how Mr. A., at
the age of eighty, still works fourteen hours a day; how this
writer and that musician did their best work after seventy.

Vanity of vanities, all is vanity! Surely Americans push
themselves and each other hard enough for most of a lifetime.
Can't we leave them alone in their later years? What's wrong
with sitting in a rocking chair on the porch, looking out at the
passers-by and looking up at the sky? Can't we even let our
senior citizens relax, let down their hair, and act their age? If
we did, they would be better grandmothers and better grandfathers.

I hope you won't regard this as nothing more than an
indictment of American society. I have merely picked out one or
two of the false values that we confront as Christian families.
Finally, let us try to see what Christian families have to do in
this kind of setting.

Christian families should surely accept with gratitude everything in their society that is good, appreciate it, support it, and
further it. At the same time, they are committed to try to change

whatever in their society is wrong. Our families are engaged with society. In the Middle Ages if you wanted to be a real Christian, you withdrew from the world into a monastery and put a wall round you, to shut yourself off from the contamination of the evil world. But this is not our way. We were told to be "in the world, yet not of the world"; this is our calling. Christian families are in the world, engaged with it, involved in it, inextricably tied up with it. And this is our task—to try constantly to raise the standards, to try constantly to let in the light. If you will examine some of these false values more closely, they all stem from the sense of bewilderment and "lostness" of people today—people without a purpose, people without direction, people without a faith. It is here that Christian families must bear their witness and do their work.

In conclusion, I want to try to give a very brief sketch of what a Christian family ought to look like in the world of our time. I think there are three distinctive marks of a Christian family, and I shall do no more than identify them.

1. The first mark is *worship*. The Christian family is a family of people who are "looking up." They are looking up because they acknowledge that they are sustained and motivated by a "power above themselves." In many old English homes, and in some American homes, I have found a card that said—"Christ is the head of this house: the unseen listener at every conversation, the unseen guest at every meal." Whether you have a card or not, this is surely the first mark of the Christian family. The Christian family seeks to do the will of God and seeks to live in the presence of Christ as Lord and Master.

This does not need necessarily to be expressed in externals. I think it is possible to overemphasize even good practices like family devotions. In East Asia, where my wife and I worked with many Christian family life movements, we discovered to our great concern that almost all that they were asking was that the people should have family devotions. And, when we looked into some of these family situations, we found they *did* have family devotions, but they weren't living Christian lives. Worship is

something that permeates the whole life of the family. It is a
constant awareness of the presence and brooding guidance of
God and the lordship of Christ. This should be the mark of
every Christian family.

2. Second, the Christian family demonstrates *fellowship*. It is
a group "whose hands are joined together," a group that
recognizes that it is at "peace within itself." But not just a peace
that comes by avoiding conflict—this is a mistake that Christian
families sometimes make. Christian families are as open to
interpersonal conflict as non-Christian families are; just as
weeds grow as much in Christians' gardens as in non-Christians'
gardens. It is not the absence of conflict that makes a Christian
family. It is that the Christian family knows how to handle
conflict. It has the means by which to resolve it. And so the
Christian family is a sort of a working model of the kingdom of
heaven.

3. Third, the Christian family is committed to *service and
witness*. It is a group of people who are looking up, a group of
people whose hands are joined, a group of people who are
"facing outward." It is a group that recognizes the power above
itself, a peace within itself, and a purpose beyond itself. The
man who prayed, "God bless me and my wife, Jim and his wife,
us four and no more. Amen," was not praying a Christian
prayer. The Christian family constantly looks outward—to serve,
to help, and to heal.

Let me close with a brief story about a friend of mine, a very
fine Christian woman named Kathleen Bliss. She and I were
undergraduates together at Cambridge. She became a distinguished Christian leader in later years, and I remember once
hearing her speak at a meeting in England at which she said: "I
was brought up in a Christian home. I can remember what it
was like as a girl to come home from school, eagerly expecting to
find my mother awaiting me; to come in and find the house
empty, to call and look everywhere for my mother and find that
she wasn't there; and then to go into the kitchen, and find a note
on the table—'Get yourself something to eat, I've gone to help a

neighbor.' " She said, "It was in this kind of experience that I realized I was a member of a Christian home. The home was not there to minister to *me*. The home was there to minister God's love, peace, and compassion to a needy world."

This kind of family living, in the midst of a bewildered and confused world, radiates a shining light. The ultimate hope that we may build the kingdom of heaven on earth lies not with the preachers, not with the theologians, not even with the missionaries, but only in the end with the development of more and more truly Christian families which will ultimately, in God's time and by his grace, multiply and eventually merge into a Christian world family.

9

Family Crises

There are so many family crises today that it would take a good while merely to enumerate them. Juvenile delinquency has tripled in the last few years. The divorce rate remains the highest that any civilized nation has ever approached. There is one broken home for every two marriage licenses. The number of unmarried mothers is a quarter of a million a year now. Venereal diseases have mounted 500 per cent in the last five years—just after we were assured that the "miracle drugs" had wiped them out. Here is another evidence that medicine isn't a substitute for morality. We are seeing a major increase in syphilis among teen-age boys. One of the facts that astounds the public health authorities is that a large part of all syphilis is now spread homosexually.

I could go on with a long list of these crises, some tragic, some a little smaller: mental and physical illnesses, accidents, alcoholism, gambling, business reverses, bankruptcy, adultery—and that most frequent, most unnecessary, most easily preventable, sometimes most fatal crisis of letting a marriage just slump down into a rut where it isn't of any value to anybody and is broken up by adultery or any other outside pressure. We can certainly avoid that. I want to limit myself to identifying a dozen crises. I think these twelve are more important than we have realized.

1. The first crisis I'll mention is the wedding, and one aspect

of it particularly—that is, that the wedding is too often merely a transition from appreciation to depreciation. We haven't begun to realize how rapidly that change takes place, in some cases almost as soon as bride and groom get outside the church. During the courtship and the betrothal period each has emphasized the good aspects of the other. They spoke to each other in praise and love. Sometimes, no doubt, fingers were crossed. The man (or woman), I am afraid, too often would think: "I certainly don't like the way she is behaving. We can't live this way the rest of our lives. This isn't the time to upset the apple cart since we are going to be married in three weeks, but after we are married that will have to stop." So each of them goes into marriage too often with reservations and prepared to have a showdown as soon as possible.

When the honeymoon is over—of course you know how to tell when the honeymoon is over—there are various formulas. One has it that the honeymoon is over when the husband takes his wife off a pedestal and puts her on a budget. But that basis is much too narrow. I think it is more correct to say that the honeymoon is over when both stop saying to each other, "Darling, you are absolutely perfect," and begin to say to each other, "The trouble with you is . . . !" That's when the feeling changes from appreciation to depreciation. It changes from an atmosphere of continual expressed admiration to an atmosphere of continual petty criticism and fault finding. A good many marriages never survive that initial period. It may drag on for years, but the damage done at that time isn't easily overcome.

All of us have seen this. I was particularly struck by it in a careful study we made at the American Institute of Family Relations of people who had come to us before marriage and to whom we had given some special education. Later on we checked to find out how they were getting along. Practically all of them were doing very well, I am happy to say. We asked them to enumerate the factors that they thought were most important in making their marriage a success. Time and again the women replied in such words as: "My husband continues to express his appreciation of me."

I don't suppose many men realize how much anxiety a woman carries into marriage, feeling that perhaps she can't live up to the responsibilities. More is expected of her in many ways than is expected of the man. Many of them worry about whether they can really make good, whether the husband won't find out that they are not at all prepared for the responsibilities. If the husband is wise and understanding, he will continue to tell his wife that she is wonderful. That helps her to be wonderful. A good many marriages are destroyed by the sudden chill that comes almost immediately after the marriage in the change from appreciation to depreciation.

2. The second crisis is one that we joke about too much but have not studied enough—the in-law problem. It's time we stopped joking about it and began to take it seriously. Judson and Mary Landis in their study of hundreds of marriages asked married couples what they found to be the greatest problem in starting marriage. Overwhelmingly, it was "getting along with in-laws."

John L. Thomas, Jesuit sociologist of St. Louis University, made a study of seven thousand divorces in the archdiocese of Chicago. If anyone still has the delusion that Roman Catholics don't get divorces, let him look at the figures. Dr. Thomas tried to identify the causes of the divorces. Many of us have done that, but we weren't smart enough to take the next step he took—that is, to correlate the cause with the length of the marriage. Obviously the factors that break up a marriage in the first few weeks might not be the same as those that break up a marriage after twenty years. He found that to be true. During the first twelve months after the wedding, he decided, the mother-in-law broke up more marriages than any other one factor. After that her influence gradually disappeared, and alcoholism took its place.

There's something seriously wrong in a situation in which the mother, who presumably loves the young people and wants them to be successful, is the one who destroys the marriage—quite unintentionally in most cases, of course. And it isn't always her fault. Sometimes the younger generation is much worse in its attitudes than the older one.

I remember a young woman who spoke to me once in Houston after a lecture, coming up, as often happens, and expecting me to solve an insoluble problem for her in thirty seconds while others were waiting to shake hands.

"What's the trouble?" I asked.

"It's my mother-in-law," she said.

"What's she done to you?"

She hesitated a moment and replied, "Well, I suppose in a sense you would say she hasn't done anything to me. That is—I have never seen her—but I just hate the idea that she exists!"

Well, that's going too far. I referred her to a psychiatrist, but I don't believe he could do anything for her unless he locked her up. She was, I am afraid, beyond human help. Certainly we can't allow this state of affairs to exist without making some effort to prevent it, and I have never known of any systematic effort to do so. We need classes for mothers-in-law. We need premarital education for mothers-in-law just as much as we do for daughters-in-law. It is one of the things the church might well take up, it seems to me. We can't afford to face with equanimity—I speak feelingly because my wife and I have four married sons—the finding of E. W. Burgess and Leonard S. Cottrell, Jr. in their study of success in marriage, that the happiest marriages are those in which the parents on both sides are dead! I don't know a sadder, more melancholy finding in all modern social science than that. It is high time to do something about it.

3. The third crisis comes with the pregnancy of the bride. We have plenty of books that deal with preparation for childbirth. Many people take good courses in the subject. But even when the birth of the first child is eagerly desired, the evidence is overwhelming that neither the husband nor the wife is really prepared for the pregnancy, psychologically. We haven't covered the ground adequately. And of course not all births are planned.

In a fourth to a third of all cases even the most educated members of the population still have unplanned pregnancies.

4. A fourth crisis involves the new father. He is the one who needs the most help, I think. The mother has been getting help for nine months. Usually the father gets none. Those who are responsible for courses in preparation for childbirth are insisting that the father come in with the mother and take as much of the course as possible. He needs it. But too often he is quite unprepared for the sudden transition he makes from number one boy to number three boy. He is just pushed into the background. It is essential that he should be, for a while at least; but the male ego doesn't take to that sort of thing. His male ego hasn't been given enough attention in our educational process. We men don't like to talk about it for obvious reasons.

Dozens of polls have been taken among women all over North America and in every civilized country asking, "What is your greatest complaint against your husband?" Overwhelmingly, unanimously every one of them comes out with the same answer—it is the egotism, the conceit, the self-satisfaction, the general self-centeredness of the husband. I'll just balance the picture by saying that the overwhelming, unanimous verdict of husbands who are asked a similar question about their wives is, "She nags me."

This ego of the male is very important, but it has become a great nuisance, as with the man who said, "Nobody can complain that I am conceited, because actually I am a great deal smarter than I think I am." So the husband may not be prepared to take second place or third place to the new baby. If the wife's mother moves in—as she is often too willing to do—to help out, then he's very much in the minority. Many a marriage has been broken up as a result of the birth of the first child, the experience that should have been the greatest factor in bringing the husband and wife together.

That is a particular danger, of course, in the interfaith marriage. Earl Emme at Bradley University in Peoria, Illinois, who made some of the most worthwhile studies of interfaith marriages, found that the major point of breakage was the birth of the first child. It might have brought husband and wife closer together if they had been orphans on a desert island, but they weren't. They had a family over here and a family over there with different backgrounds, each thinking that its member had made a serious mistake in getting tied up with the other crowd.

Couples in many interfaith marriages are not adequately prepared. They don't face before they marry certain problems that are inescapable. They stall along until the birth of the first baby. Then they can't stall any longer because the parents move in.

The wife's mother says, "Of course we're going to have Dr. Fisher baptize the baby on Easter."

"No, my husband's family thinks the child shouldn't be baptized until he gets to be around fourteen years of age," her daughter replies.

"Don't you think we are going to stand for that for one minute," mother snorts. "This is our only grandchild, and we're not going to tolerate that sort of business."

The two families clash, head-on, and the young father and mother end in separation, a tragedy that ought to have been prevented by preparation in advance.

5. A fifth crisis is the failure of each sex to understand the other, due to the fact that they are male and female respectively. They differ in every possible way. They differ literally in every cell in their bodies. They have, in large and important areas of life, different standards of value. They think differently, eat differently, drink differently, talk differently, walk differently, spend their money differently.

I'm particularly concerned right now with the fact that they talk differently. I won't claim that's because they differ in every cell in their bodies, giving them different inheritances. In any of these widespread and interesting sex differences, it is difficult—indeed it is impossible—to say how much is due to inborn nature and how much of it merely to education. We all sympathize with the uncertainty of the boy who brought home from school a very bad report card which he handed to his father, saying, "It's terrible, isn't it, dad? What do you think's the matter with me—heredity or environment?" These are inseparable. All we can say is probably a little of each. But the fact is that men and women don't use the same language. At least they don't use the same words to mean the same thing.

A girl says to her friend, "What do you think of Alice?"

The friend says, "She's sweet, isn't she?"

The girl says, "I don't like her either."

That is understood by women. Men think it doesn't make sense. It is not intended to make sense to a man. Many things that women say aren't intended to make sense to a man. They are like diplomatic language, concealing thoughts for some entirely different purpose. Since that is the purpose of language from her point of view, a woman is continually in difficulty because the husband doesn't have the same idea of what language is for.

A French psychiatrist, Maurice Poirot, writes on this very interestingly. He carries it a little too far, but he claims that many of the difficulties that women get into are due to the fact that they don't believe a man is telling the truth when he is telling the truth. The man tells the woman he doesn't intend to marry her. That's a plain statement, but not for her. She is going to spend weeks now figuring just what he had in mind. What was his purpose in saying that? What was back of that? What did he really mean by that? What he really meant was that he didn't intend to marry her. But she knows she would never have laid her cards on the table that way. "Laying the cards on the table" is a masculine phrase. It doesn't exist in a woman's vocabulary. Laying her cards on the table isn't the way she plays the game. So women get into difficulties because they can't realize that a man isn't trying to deceive them. Dr. Poirot says man is too naive and simple-minded to be able to. Whatever the reason, he is very likely to make a truthful statement which his wife won't take as such. Men never can win in this game.

You remember the man who kissed his wife in the morning and said, "Good-by, sugar." When he came home at night she wasn't at the door to meet him. He found her in the kitchen crying.

"What's the matter, honey?"

"Nothing."

"Must be something wrong."

"No."

After half an hour's cross examination, she finally admitted that when he left in the morning he called her sugar.

"Sure, darling, that's right. You are the sweetest thing in the world."

"No," she sobbed, "I looked it up in the dictionary, and another meaning of sugar is *any evaporated sap.*"

The different languages that men and women use create a perpetual crisis in any family. We need to take a little more time to educate husbands and wives at this point.

6. The sixth crisis is in meeting the need for sex education when it first arises—and that's about the age of three or four years, far before parents are at all ready to face it in most cases. And they don't face it. Studies show that not more than 50 per cent of all mothers and 25 per cent of all fathers give their children anything that children can recognize as rudimentary sex education.

There has been a little improvement in that. Some fathers are trying to do better. Two men were bragging about what good fathers they were. One of them said, "I've already told my son about the bees and the flowers." The other said, "I told my son about the bees and the flowers too, but I didn't want to go too fast. I used artificial flowers."

This need to meet the child's requirement of sex education when it first arises is one we haven't begun to face frankly. The problem starts with the birth of the child, or maybe even long before with the marriage of the father and the mother. The importance of the relationship between father and mother needs emphasis. This is one of the many cases in which example is more important than precept. Few things are more necessary in the sex education of the child than his seeing his father and mother express love to each other. The father ought to explain to the children as they get older why he loves their mother, describing her good points. But he doesn't show his love for the mother in the presence of the children—and sometimes not even in the presence of the mother.

The strong, silent man who refuses to tell his wife he loves her, because, he says, "I told her that when I asked her to marry me and it holds good until revoked," is a menace not only to himself and his wife but to his children also. Some very interesting surveys show that the children who grow up to make the most successful marriages and who have the most successful sex adjustments in their own marriages are the children whose fathers and mothers not only loved each other, but were rather demonstrative in expressing it to each other in the presence of the children.

Here we run up against another of the peculiarities of the male sex. The taboo on tenderness in males is largely peculiar to Anglo-Saxons. The feeling on the part of men that they mustn't show any tenderness to anybody is extremely damaging to marriage. Women want in husbands a lot of things but primarily strength, tenderness, and companionship. In a Christian home they ought to get all these qualities in abundance. In a good many homes of all kinds they don't, but at least the husband could show some tenderness. If he did it would change the whole life of his children in many cases.

7. The seventh crisis, one of the most serious problems of modern times and one of the many we don't like to talk about, is homosexuality. We have no place in this country for five or six million male homosexuals who are becoming more aggressive all the time. They are coming out of hiding now. They are beginning to demand their "rights," as they call them.

It isn't easy, although it can be done, to "cure" them once they are established. It is relatively easy to prevent the development of homosexuality. So far as the boys are concerned, the evidence is becoming more and more overwhelming that homosexuals can't grow up in a home where husband and wife love each other, where both love their children, and where the father has a warm relationship with his son as well as with his wife. It's a sure prevention and doesn't cost a cent. It ought to be made universal.

8. An eighth crisis is likely to appear when girls begin to go steady. In the widespread perversion of normal social life that we have permitted, this may begin as early as the sixth grade. Little attempt is made to provide them with an adequate social life that will prevent going steady. It will take effort to change this dating pattern of adolescents; but it can be done if we want to make the effort and if we'll "gang up" on the young people, so to speak, by concerted action on the part of parents, school, PTAs, churches, and youth organizations. It is relatively easy to see how it can be done, and it would not be too difficult to do, if we want to do it. If we don't do it, we'll continue to have a lot of these premature marriages with all the difficulties that they involve.

Last year in the United States four thousand girls married at the age of fourteen or under. You and I know perfectly well that the girl doesn't live, never lived in this country, who at the age of fourteen is prepared for marriage. It is no credit to Christians or any other kind of civilization to have marriages of that sort.

9. The ninth crisis I want to identify appears in the adolescent years when boys begin to encounter female aggressiveness for which they are not prepared. I am not overlooking the danger to the girl from male aggressiveness. We talk so much about that, we recognize it so well, that we haven't realized how another situation has in a sense slipped up on us. The problem is one of female aggressiveness and masculine passiveness. Even a generation ago M. W. Peck and F. L. Wells in their study of the "psycho-sexual development," as they called it, of Harvard graduate students found that of the minority who had had premarital sexual experience, most were victims of seduction by

older and more-experienced women. Some states have very properly made statutory rape apply to both sexes. There certainly should be an age of consent under which a boy would be protected from the virtual attacks of older and more aggressive females.

Among the teen-age boys who have been coming to the Los Angeles city clinic by the hundreds with infectious syphilis in the last three or four years, it is found that the majority were infected by older and more experienced and aggressive women who were virtually seducing them. We will have to recognize this as a phase of the education for citizenship and for life that we have been missing almost completely. Historically and traditionally, it has been the male who has been expected to take the initiative in relations with the other sex. One of our greatest challenges is to set up educational measures by which boys can be taught that the evidence of their virility is in the protection of women and not in the exploitation of women.

Unfortunately, evidence accumulating over a whole generation now shows a peculiar inversion of what we have considered normal response. I think the latest proof was a survey by a Madison Avenue research corporation to determine which television programs would capture the greatest male audience. Male viewers, the report declared, seemed to respond much more enthusiastically when women in the commercials make the advances. The ads that scored best were those in which women took the amorous initiative rather than the men.

10. The tenth crisis occurs in middle life when the curves of sexual desire on the part of husband and wife cross. I have been astonished, in reading the large correspondence I get, to find how often this seems to be the basic difficulty. The man's sexual drive is declining steadily, as I showed in a pioneer study nearly thirty years ago on this point. It is highest just before he is old enough to vote, and there is a gradual slowing down until theoretical extinction at the age of seventy-seven, which means that as many continued after that as stopped earlier. For a variety of reasons, the woman's interest in sexual relations

frequently increases from the time of marriage onward; so quite often after fifteen, twenty, or twenty-five years of marriage the lines cross. The husband is losing interest at the same time the wife is gaining interest. Understanding the reason for this leads easily to remedying the difficulty, but failure to understand it leads to conflict which frequently undermines the whole foundation of the marriage.

11. The eleventh crisis occurs after the last child leaves home. We all know something about that, because it is talked about, and we see it on all sides. Everyone is familiar with the breakup of a marriage after twenty or twenty-five years of what was thought to be a successful relationship. We say, "Why, the Smiths are getting a divorce. Goodness! They have been married a quarter of a century. If they could get along together for twenty-five years, certainly they should get along a little longer. I can't imagine what the trouble is." If we could see behind the scenes we might find that there hasn't been anything to hold that marriage together for a long time except the children. All the other interests they should have built up weren't built up or they died out. They still could talk about the children and plan for them, but now the last child is gone and the wife in particular finds that her life is empty. The woman with any foresight at all plans for this. But too many don't, and they get into difficulty. When her last daughter, for whom she has planned so long, of whose marriage she has thought and schemed so long, is gone, a mother often feels completely bereaved.

As her daughter left on her honeymoon, one such mother turned to her husband and, throwing herself on his shoulder and weeping, said, "I don't know what I'll do now." The husband replied, "Why don't you try being married?"

We ought to build up these marriages earlier in life, and the church is a good place in which to build them. There we can help the couple to find something to do together. With a moderate amount of intelligent planning, the husband and wife can experience their best years in the 47 per cent of their married life which comes after the last child leaves home.

12. The twelfth crisis is the rapidly increasing and tragic tendency to let sexual relations begin before the wedding day. It has become such a part of our mores now that books put out by men and women who ought to know better are urging that premarital sex is desirable. Christian young people are assured that it is entirely proper, that "love"—whatever that may be—is the only thing that counts. Over the past quarter of a century random studies have shown that 20, 30, 40, or even 50 per cent of the brides were pregnant when they took their marriage vows.

Psychiatrist Horace Grey made a study of all the marriage licenses issued in one California county over a period of seventeen months and then followed it up with the reports of births to these couples. He found that, if the conventional period of 288 days is taken as the actual length of gestation, 47 per cent of all the brides under twenty years of age were pregnant on the wedding day. In fact, one in every five was three months pregnant.

This situation is unsatisfactory from every point of view. It represents a tragic failure in our education for marriage and parenthood. It demands a concerted attack from all who take the American home seriously.

10

How Can We Help?

There are many ways in which we can help other people. Why not get out and do so? Counseling is a direct and important method of helping. Historically this has been a function of the church. However, the church has been pushed out of counseling to some extent in recent years. It is beginning to come back now, and I shall suggest a number of aspects that we can think about together.

John W. Drakeford of Southwestern Baptist Theological Seminary at Fort Worth, in his book *Counseling for Church Leaders,* gives many illustrations of the historical function of the church right back—not quite to Adam and Eve (who needed a little counseling themselves) , but back to the Old Testament, pointing out that counseling is what the church has always done. Traditionally, the clergymen were the counselors of the communities. It is only in the last generation or so that the psychiatrist particularly and perhaps the psychologist secondarily as a "me, too," enterprise made some attempt to supplant the minister, calling him an intruder, when obviously they are the intruders themselves.

Just for the sake of argument, I would say that everyone is a counselor whether he wants to be or not, whether he knows it or not. Counseling is a universal form of communication. The largest part of counseling is probably done by parents with their children or by wives with their husbands, according to the general opinion of the male sex. A man can make a mistake without knowing it, they say, but not if he is married. Every teacher is a counselor, every social worker, executives of all sorts of organizations, every Boy Scout leader. You can hardly find anyone who isn't doing counseling; and if he isn't doing it as well as he ought to, then he needs to work harder.

Most counseling is indirect. Of course, the most successful counseling is probably that given by example. Gilbert Wrenn, well-known contemporary psychologist, says counseling is a way of living with all persons with whom you come in contact. We are counseling merely by being with people, by living with them, even more than by what we say. We need more of that kind of counseling.

What are the qualities needed to make a good counselor? The first thing we have to recognize is that counseling is essentially an art and not a science. I don't mean there isn't a science underlying every art, but everyone who writes on the subject agrees that counseling is essentially an art.

The artist in the first place has an aptitude for his subject. If he hasn't, he doesn't get very far. In the second place, he spends his life working hard at his art, practicing it, associating with good artists, seeing good art, devoting his time to it. And if he works hard enough, he gets somewhere.

It is exactly the same with counseling. Success in counseling is 51 per cent aptitude and 49 per cent experience, if you want to put figures on it. Scientific degrees and membership in scientific societies have very little to do with it.

If you want to ask how to become an artist of any kind, it's a little difficult to say. If you want to know how to become a musician, you will be told that first you have to be born with some musical talent. If you are born tone deaf, don't start. But if you do have some talent, then you simply study, work, practice, practice, practice—and practice is a large part of the game—and you become a musician. It isn't so easy, then, to tell anybody in detail how he can become a satisfactory musician.

It is easy, however, to list some of the ways you can't be a good counselor. Let's look at it for a moment from this negative point of view.

1. In the first place, if you want to be a good counselor one of the prerequisites to helping other people solve their problems is to solve your own problems. Now, of course, that is a counsel of perfection that excludes all of us. But anyone who has serious emotional or moral problems will do well to clear those up before he tries to pull the mote out of his brother's eye. There are some professional counselors whom you wouldn't want as intimate friends of your family. It is one of the points on which we should demand that the counseling profession take a more direct stand; that it cease to push forward people who are morally unworthy of recognition. But to the extent that you have any unsolved problems of a serious nature, it is a good thing to be able at least to identify them and to get to work on them.

2. Another way in which you are barred from counseling is to be aggressive. You have to be energetic. There is a sharp distinction. The reigning dogma for ten or twelve years was the nondirective or so-called client-centered type of counseling, in which the counselor wasn't expected to say anything except "yes" or "I see" or something of that sort, and force the client to do all the talking, solve his own problems. The theory was that somehow, in some mysterious way, deep down inside him the client had the solution to the problem, and all he had to be allowed to do was get it out.

If he had had the solution, he wouldn't have come to see you. He wouldn't have wasted his time. That type of counseling was largely a waste of time. On the other hand, if you are aggressive you put the client on the defensive. Then he is fighting you instead of fighting his own problems, and you are wasting time. Many counselors make this mistake.

3. A third handicap is a "Jehovah complex," and that bars all of us. Counseling leads one, too often, to feel that he is a little finer clay than the rest of mankind, that he holds the fate of other people in his hand, that he has access to secret information

that nobody else has. It is an intoxicating feeling, and it requires continual watching. Everyone who is doing counseling in any way ought to get down on his knees every morning and pray to be protected from a Jehovah complex. Then he ought to get down on his knees again every evening and pray to be forgiven for the one he has had all day, because he isn't going to avoid this universal temptation. But to the extent that you are on the watch for it, you can save yourself. One professional counselor has his desk on a little platform about one foot above the floor. The client sits down there, looking up at the great white throne and appealing for mercy. No doubt this makes the counselor feel important, but it isn't counseling.

4. In the fourth place, a counselor must be respected. One of the best recent books on the subject is *Persuasion and Healing* by Jerome Frank, professor of psychiatry at Johns Hopkins University. One of the points he makes is that the techniques of counseling are widely used. They are much the same techniques, whether it is Soviet brainwashing, psychoanalysis, the medicine man in the primitive tribe, or a dozen other forms. In all cases success depends very largely on the client's expecting to be helped due to the respect he has for the counselor. The minister in particular enjoys prestige, and this gives him an advantage others don't have.

5. In the fifth place, and another point Dr. Frank emphasizes, is emotional warmth. The tradition of the psychoanalyst was that the counselor was entirely aloof. He would never think of showing any particular feeling for the client, or having friendly relations with him outside. He was sort of an IBM machine, so to speak. Now that's all nonsense. It's entirely possible to be too emotionally warm in the sense of backslapping and buddy-buddy fellowship. It is just as well to keep the relationship on a professional basis. But unless the client feels, "Here's someone who is friendly," you can't do much.

Don't sympathize with the client. It is natural to suppose that you ought to. Ministers particularly are very sympathetic or perhaps they wouldn't be ministers or wouldn't stay in the ministry very long. We have at the Institute a personality test, the Johnson Temperament Inventory. One of the traits it measures is sympathy. As a vocational adaptation, we find that ministers almost universally rank high in sympathy. For that reason they are frequently imposed upon. They are too sympathetic.

Sympathy means sharing the feeling of the individual. The minute you share his feeling, you put yourself in his place. You say to yourself unconsciously, "It is perfectly natural for him to feel that way; I'd feel the same way if I were he." You share the individual's grief if he has lost a partner. In his place you would feel as he does. Now you can't afford to do that in counseling, because the client is coming with problems which don't represent something that you ought to *feel with*. He is wrong; that is why he has come to you. If you simply let him see that you sympathize with him, then he goes out and says: "Well, I guess I am all right. I thought I was in the wrong, but he seems to sympathize with me. Why, I am sure, from the way he behaved and talked, that if he were in my place he would not only have done the same, but he would have done twice as bad as I did. I guess there's no need for me to make any change." You can't afford to sympathize with a client in counseling.

What is wanted, of course, to use the technical word that everyone knows now, is empathy. Not feeling *with* but feeling *into*. Empathy is a little more than intellectually understanding. You put yourself in the client's place to the extent of understanding why he feels that way, but not sharing it yourself. If you have empathy, you have one of the great qualifications in counseling. Unfortunately, there's no test by which we can determine in advance whether one has empathy. We are looking for one; and if we can ever find one, it will help to select better counselors.

6. Then the counselor has to be resourceful. In present theory the major key to counseling is to get the client into action. We must get him to do something, along right lines, of course.

The psychoanalysts put all their weight on giving him insight. That doesn't go far. Indeed, insight sometimes does him harm. It simply lets him revolve in a little circle inside of his own misfortune. Franz Alexander, who is perhaps the leading psychoanalyst in the country, said, "Insight doesn't produce action, but action produces insight." You get your client into action, and he begins to understand by right action why he was unhappy when he was in the wrong action. But if you simply help him to see that he is making a big mistake, you are telling him the one thing he already knows. What he wants to learn is, "What am I going to do about it? Why don't you tell me how I can get out of it?" So listening isn't enough. Listening is the thing to do when the client first comes in. You have to give him a chance to tell his story fully. It takes time. Counseling is a time-consuming job.

In Oklahoma City there is an institution known as the Oklahoma City Family Clinic. It is in its seventeenth year now. The *Reader's Digest* published an article about it, as have various newspapers and magazines. It is a clinic which was set up as a nonprofit volunteer agency. The panel consists of four persons: a minister, a lawyer, a physician, and a financial expert. At the beginning of each year the council of churches selects a panel of ministers they think suitable for this purpose from which the clinic can draw. The Bar Association does this for lawyers, the Medical Society for physicians, and the Retail Merchant's Association presents a list of financiers. Several of these are presidents or vice-presidents of banks, some of the best-known people in the community. Others are credit raters. These people understand just why the client is in financial difficulty. He heard about "no money down and thirty years to pay."

The panel takes one from each of these professions, and it is an interesting restriction that no one is ever taken who volunteers for the job. If you want the job, they don't want you. They think that means you are probably a do-gooder, perhaps have some ax to grind, some particular cure-all you want to work off. They take those who are nominated by the societies, and they bring the couple before them. The wife is given a chance to tell the counselors her whole story. This is likely to take an hour and a half. She comes in wound up, and she has to be allowed to run down without an interruption. Then her husband has a chance to tell his story. I am citing this to remind you that if you are going to do some listening, you have to listen. You have not only to have "listening ears" but big ones and plenty of time. You can't hurry people in a matter like this, so don't do all the talking yourself. Do a reasonable amount of listening first, but after that get your client into action.

7. Another point at which the counselor has to be careful is not to condemn. You don't want to sympathize, you don't want to be unsympathetic, but you don't want to be condemnatory, either. It is difficult for us to watch ourselves at this point. The client tells a story of moral wrong that he has done. We see the result clearly. We are not just going to denounce him. That won't help him. But we feel we owe it to ourselves to let him understand that we don't accept that standard. The minute you do that—and he is very keen to see what your attitude is—you have probably lost him. He says to himself, "I thought he would understand me. I thought he would see my difficulty, but like all the others, all he could do was say that I was wrong, that I was a sinner. I knew that before I came in, and that's why I went—to see what to do about it. No use for me to go there if all he is going to do is tell me that I am a poor, miserable wretch. I won't go back to him."

8. There's another point at which many fall into a trap and that's to ask the client to do something for the counselor's sake. We want to motivate him; we want to get him to act. This problem of motivation may be 51 per cent of all counseling, and it is too often ignored in discussions of the subject. The client frequently knows before he comes in, just as well as he does afterward, what's wrong with him. He knows frequently what he ought to do. Somebody has to motivate him to do it, and that's our job. But how are we going to do it?

It is easy to say: "Now, Jim, you certainly are in trouble. You are a miserable failure. Everybody who knows you is down on you. You haven't a friend in the world. Anybody who tried to help you, you have just kicked him in the teeth. There isn't anybody who will hold out a hand to pull you out of the ditch where you are putting yourself—except me. Jim, I believe in you. I am going to stand by you, Jim. I am the only friend you have. Now you go out and do right for my sake." Well, if he does it for your sake, you have harmed him rather than helped him. You may have kept him from committing that particular offense a second time, but you have also taught him that he doesn't need to do anything because it is right but merely because somebody makes an emotional appeal to him. He does what you tell him to, "for your sake." You have made a strong emotional appeal.

A month later another old friend comes along and says: "Jim, the baby needs shoes, and my wife hasn't got a summer dress. We've got to rob the bank to get some money. I depend on you, Jim. Help me now, for my sake. You will do this for me, won't you?" So, of course, Jim goes right along and does it because you have taught him that the thing to do is what anybody tells him to with a strong emotional appeal.

9. Then, of course, you should not solve the client's problems for him. Usually, we can see immediately what needs to be done, and it is easy simply to tell him what to do. We can see in our opinion that he ought to get a divorce, or more frequently that he ought not to get a divorce, and we can just tell him so. That isn't helping him. The purpose of counseling is to teach him how to solve his own problems. If you solve them for him, then you hurt him again. You have taught him not to try to solve his problems but to go to somebody else and let somebody else solve them for him. The problem is to help the individual figure out what he ought to do in such a way that he recognizes that he has accepted that course of action as the logical thing from his own point of view.

For example, I never tell people they ought to get a divorce; I never tell people they oughtn't to get a divorce. They have to settle that for themselves. I can help them, but they have to make the decision. A woman comes in with a long sob story: "Dr. Popenoe, I can't go any longer; I have reached the limit. It's intolerable. I have come to the conclusion that the only thing to do is to get a divorce." Well, I know that isn't what she came to me for. I can't get a divorce for her. If she wants a divorce, she wouldn't waste her time coming to see me. She would go to one of the divorce lawyers who would get her a divorce so fast it would make her head swim. She comes to me because she wants to know what to do and wants to talk it over with somebody.

I say, not in so many words: "Really, I never saw you before and may never see you again, and from one point of view it doesn't make the slightest difference to me whether you get a divorce or not. But since you tell me you have seven years invested in this marriage and have two children, even though, as you say, it seems to be absolutely intolerable, the fact that you have survived seven years indicates that probably it won't kill you to take seven days longer or even seven weeks. Let's take a little time to look through this and see all sides of it so that when you make your decision—and you have to make your decision, nobody can make it for you—it will be the right one for you. Then you won't say ten years from now, as so many people do, 'If I had known ten years ago what I know now, I would have done something different.'" That sounds reasonable to her, and so we simply think through it, look all around it. I can suggest things that she probably hasn't been willing to think of and force her to think of them. In no time at all, the answer is perfectly obvious.

The answer is not always so obvious as it was in the case of a Canadian schoolteacher who wrote me. She hated teaching school and wanted to quit. She thought the only way she could quit teaching school was to marry, and there was a man who wanted to marry her. She asked me to tell her whether or not she ought to marry him. I replied: "I have never seen you and never will see you. Don't ask me to tell you whether you ought to marry him. I wouldn't do that even if I knew you well, but I'll help you to clarify your own thought. You write me again and make a list of the reasons why you should marry him and the reasons why you shouldn't marry him, if there are any reasons of either kind. I'll help you think through it, and you can use your own judgment." She wrote back promptly. She had two parallel columns. Under "why she should marry him" there was only one reason—she wanted to quit teaching. Under "why she shouldn't marry him" there were three reasons: (1) she was very much ashamed of his manners and appearance; (2) she would be terribly ashamed to introduce him to any of her friends; (3) she couldn't bear the thought of having him touch her. She added, "Dr. Popenoe, this is the end of the correspondence."

It's not often that the situation is as absurd as it was in that case, but if you let a client make parallel columns it is often a very satisfactory way of counseling, I assure you. There's nothing new about it, but it saves time. You can suggest, "Have you thought of the financial difficulties; have you thought of the loss of your social life, or most of it? Social life in America is built on married couples. If you are no longer married, you are going to find that there's less activity available to you." It doesn't take long for her to say: "It is perfectly obvious I don't want a divorce. Just show me how to avoid it. I am willing to do anything you say."

10. In the next place, don't be a perfectionist. We always think we ought to make a complete cure. We want to have the individual go out leaping, rejoicing, and praising the Lord for the miracle that has been worked. It doesn't happen that way. The physician can't do that. He has to do the best he can. He can't save the man's leg; he has to cut it off. He can give him an artificial leg. This is better than no leg at all, and it is far better than the one he had that was going to kill him when gangrene spread. We frequently have to be satisfied with partial success.

11. In the next place, remember that counseling is a growth process. It is going to be slow. Frequently we don't get the

answers right away. We think the client represents a complete failure, but we have started him in the right direction. The next time we see him he has worked the problem out.

That's true equally of marriage counseling, which is a growth experience. Two people start in at marriage side by side. Gradually they drift farther and farther apart. When they come to us they are very far apart. However, we see them a few times—six times is our standard. When they leave, perhaps they seem to be just as far apart as they were when they came in. But what has happened is that their course has altered slightly. They are still just as far apart, but their direction has changed. Now as they go on, instead of going farther apart, they are coming together. In a year, two or three years maybe, they have come back together completely because you started them off in that direction. It is one of the big satisfactions the counselor has. We are bound to have many disappointments and failures. It is pleasant to have a few successes when you don't expect them.

In my beginning days there were several cases where I thought, not only is a divorce inevitable, but it is desirable. It is wrong to keep this couple together. They should never have married. They should not be allowed to stay together. It is a sinful thing to have this marriage in existence. I would say to myself, Paul, why don't you be sensible? There's nothing you can do here. Let them get out of this as fast as they can. And I agreed with them on the desirability of divorce. Twice when I did that, within a year or two afterward I met each of those couples on the street walking arm in arm, beaming happiness. They came over and shook my hand and said, "Dr. Popenoe, you just don't know how happy we are, and we owe it all to you. We never could be thankful enough to you for the advice you gave us." I not only felt like a fool, but I was certain that I was a fool. Whatever forms my foolishness might take in the future, I resolved that I would never make that mistake again. I never advise anybody to get a divorce.

12. Finally, don't depend on telling your own experience. Don't say, "That's the way I did it," or "Oh, when I was in

college I did a lot worse," and so forth. It is always easy to do that. We call up our own experiences partly because we think it helps to encourage them. They will think, "If he was as bad as that, I guess I am no worse than the rest of the crowd."

Don't waste your time on it. It isn't counseling at all. It is just showing off, I suppose. If you are doing anything, you are counseling yourself. Keep yourself out of it. It is desirable to cite the general experience of mankind, especially in scientific form. You can say the statistics show that in such a case as this there is only one chance in twenty that you will succeed, or whatever the fact may be. Don't go on to narrate your own history.

Now with those remarks on how not to be a counselor and some of the things you can avoid, let's consider a little more specifically the process of marriage counseling. It is much needed in most parts of the country. The higher divorce rate states are the Pacific Coast, Rocky Mountain, and Southwestern states. The situation is intolerable there. On the other hand, the South Atlantic states have low divorce rates. A good deal of interest could be drawn from a study of them.

South Carolina for something like a century and a half had no divorce. It was forbidden in the state constitution. Then the abrogation of that feature of the constitution was jammed through. If there had been a great demand for divorce, you would expect that when the brakes were taken off, the courts would be filled with suffering couples looking for relief, wouldn't you? Almost nobody showed up. There wasn't such a demand for divorce. They were getting along better than the rest of us. I published a study of this subject. There were a number of indications that family life in South Carolina was happier than in many other states of the union, and divorce was forbidden in the state constitution.

Many people said, "They just go to North Carolina or Georgia. They don't have to get one here—just go across the border." All right, what kind of a divorce rate did North Carolina and Georgia have? Next to South Carolina, they were the lowest in the country. If Georgia was providing divorces for two states, itself and South Carolina, it would have a high divorce rate, certainly. But it wasn't even having as high a divorce rate as the next state to the west. This whole matter of divorce needs to be thought through more realistically. The divorce rates in the Pacific Coast, Rocky Mountain, and Southwestern states are absurdly high. Nobody can believe we need as much divorce as that.

Marriage counseling, then, is needed, and the minister is in a good position to counsel, and so are many church members. Ministers need help from others. They have their hands pretty full already. Some ministers tell me they spend about a third of their time in counseling. It's not easy to do that and keep other things going. He is going to have to call on some of the mature adults in the congregation to help him, and they should be given some training for that purpose. Wayne Oates and John Drakeford emphasize this in their books. This is the line along which counseling is going to develop.

How are we going to start counseling the unhappy marriage? One easy way is to ask, What does a good marriage look like? We have plenty of evidence on that. A successful marriage, in general, and there are many studies to prove it, is one in which the husband and wife have much in common—common background, common ideals, common habits, religion, table manners, educational level. The more they have in common, the more likely the marriage is to be a success. If there are points in which they differ, they must sympathize at least with each other's aims and interests. But generally, the more they have in common the better off they are. If they differ in anything they themselves think is important, whether you or I think it is important or not, then they have an area of disharmony. From that point of view, then, the happily married persons have much in common and the unhappy marriage has dissimilarities where there ought to be similarities. Where those dissimilarities exist, change them into similarities and you have the job done.

That isn't the whole story but actually in a majority of cases that simple procedure is enough to do the job. You don't need to psychoanalyze. Frequently it does harm. So, while the woman is telling her story in seven reels with added sound effects, look between the lines to see where she and her husband differ; and it doesn't take very long to find that. It doesn't take long to figure out what they could do to change the differences into resemblances. Then get them into action.

Most of the differences exist in one or more of a half dozen areas. I'll just mention these without going into them fully and without any regard to the order of importance:

1. Social and recreational life is extremely important, and, of course, very easily found through the church. The young married couples' classes, which have developed so rapidly in the last twenty-five or thirty years, have been lifesavers for hundreds of thousands of marriages because they give a couple coming into a new community a ready-made social life, the kind they need.

2. Handling the finances.

3. Managing the children.

4. Managing the in-laws.

5. Sexual adjustment.

6. The wife's need for self-expression outside the home. Every wife must have some absorbing interest outside the home—not absorbing enough to make her neglect the home, but absorbing enough so that she doesn't feel that she is "just a housewife." She must have some individuality, some personality. Many women make themselves martyrs to their children, feeling that it is a virtuous thing to do. The children could profit by a little judicious neglect, if necessary, to get the mother into a better frame of mind. We almost have to dynamite her out of the house sometimes. Get her out of the home and get her, for example, to join the church and sing in the choir. Then she isn't "just a housewife" any longer. Then she isn't just Mr. Smith's wife. Then she isn't just the mother of the Smith kids. She's our new soprano. She is somebody in her own right, and she can feel much better satisfied with herself. And when she feels better satisfied with herself, everybody else is satisfied with her. The

home should be the center of her interest but not the circumference of her interest. This is equally true of the husband, of course. It is one of the points on which almost every marriage needs counseling.

In these six areas, see where the husband and wife don't think alike, and you will quickly have the direction in which to apply a little resourcefulness and some suggestions. The counselor must be resourceful. He has to supply the imagination and the resourcefulness that the client lacks. If the client had them, he wouldn't be a client. You don't tell the client what to do. You tell him how to do it. With a thorough knowledge of the resources of the community, you have to figure out what can be done and suggest that it can be done. Encourage the couple to get into action. If you do that, the first thing you know they are getting along better.

11

The Broken Home

When we consider special problems of the family, the subject is almost as broad as human nature. It is difficult to know where to start or stop. I may ignore some of the things that you think are by far the most significant in this area of the broken home. As a basis for our discussions, I am going to touch on some of those matters that seem to me to be particularly important in counseling.

I'll start with the death of a member of the family. One of the problems we always face is explaining death. Pastors have more experience in this than I have. One of the questions that is continually debated is whether a man or woman about to die should be told that the end is approaching. Many people feel that it is kinder to conceal the fact. I feel very strongly that if there is really no hope, the honest and helpful course is to tell the individual that the end is near. He can then make all necessary dispositions for this world and the next. It seems to me to be entirely childish to keep him in ignorance. One does have to be careful not to cause undue alarm.

The death of a parent is something the children have to face, and there we get into difficulties. One of our problems is that the surviving parent and relatives are chagrined because the child doesn't appear to show any grief. That is perfectly natural. The child doesn't show grief in the sense that the parent does, and probably shouldn't do so. He often seems to go ahead with very little realization of what has happened; and the idea that we should try to inflict on him the necessity of demonstrating grief, which actually he isn't mature enough to feel, may do harm.

Another point is the common tendency, if there is a surviving boy in the family, to say, "Johnnie, from now on you are the man of the family; you will have to be the father." That is dangerous. The boy isn't the man of the family. He can't be; he ought not to be; it would be disastrous if he tried to be. He ought to be protected from suggestions of that sort which may weigh too heavily on his mind and make him feel inadequate and inferior and guilty because he can't live up to what he thinks people expect of him.

The other end of the spectrum is a surviving elderly parent. In three-fourths of all cases, the father dies first. He is usually older than his wife; and women live longer than men. There are eight million widows in the nation. What will the surviving mother do? Too often the sons or daughters think they must tell Mother to come live with them. I am going to argue that this is usually the most unsatisfactory course. It is much better to encourage the mother to continue in her own home, even if it is a thousand miles away, to live with her peers and keep busy. Many of them are quite healthy enough to take a job or at least to take some active part in the world. To pull them out of a situation where they feel comfortable and familiar and bring them into a new home where they can't help feeling they are supernumeraries is usually no kindness and frequently a great injustice to all concerned. This problem of the aged parent is a painful one. In a good many ways we handle it badly, partly through misplaced kindness. It is one we ought to be prepared to meet. There are fortunately many good books on the subject, and we ought to make use of them.

The home broken by divorce involves even more serious difficulties. Adultery is by no means the only reason for a broken home—statistically not the major reason, but it is one that is pushed to the fore and is one we have to face. David Mace has been lecturing and publishing his belief that adultery of itself shouldn't be made a ground for divorce. That is quite contrary to tradition. But he thinks, and most of us would agree, that adultery, in many instances, is simply a symptom of marriage gone wrong, and that the supposed innocent partner may be actually the more guilty. I hope no one believes that he can infallibly distinguish between the innocent and the guilty party in a divorce caused by adultery. Sometimes it may seem clear, but in many cases the overt offender is actually the less guilty of the two. Time and again the wife tells the husband, "You'll have no further sexual relations with me." With maybe twenty-five or thirty years of marriage ahead, he is tempted to go somewhere else for gratification, and after a while he does. Then she raises a cry to high heaven. Who is responsible? I don't justify him at all, but is she entirely free from responsibility? Can she be considered such an innocent individual that all the sympathy is on her side?

How are we going to prepare the children who are victims of divorce? Frequently here is where most of the damage is done. I don't believe you can have divorce and a home broken in that sense without damage to the children.

Three-fourths of the time it is the wife who files for divorce. Several surveys of divorced women asked, "When difficulties arose, which of you first used the word 'divorce'; which of you insisted on it?" Three-fourths of the time the women answered, "I did."

In the counseling services I think it is certainly true that three-fourths of the time it is the wife who comes first, not necessarily because she has more to complain about than the husband—perhaps very much less, but because marriage in many ways is more important to the wife. She is more in the center of it. If the situation becomes uncomfortable, the husband can simply slide out from under. He can leave earlier in the morning, and soon he is getting his breakfast on the way downtown. He can come back later at night, and soon he is getting his dinner downtown. Then he is coming back just in time to go to bed, and finally he comes back late and goes to bed on the couch in the living room. The worse things get, the faster and farther he can slide out. The wife is right in the middle of it all the time. She is the one who is ready to explode and do something either constructive or destructive.

Unfortunately, too often she claims that she is getting a divorce for the benefit of the children. As far as she is concerned, if it were herself alone, she would let that brute kill her if he wanted to—and she knows that he does. But she just doesn't think it is right for the children to have the example of a person like that in the home. Well, I don't think any one will be convinced by that argument, but she is going to file for divorce just the same.

Incidentally, a large proportion of divorce cases never go before a judge. Thirty-five per cent of all divorce suits are never tried. They are withdrawn before they actually get into court. Often they are just a threat, a desperate effort on the part of the wife to force her husband to do something. She thinks perhaps that will have some effect. Sometimes the wife is stampeded into divorce proceedings by overzealous friends and relatives, and in many cases she has a good reason for complaint—both of them have—but after the divorce is filed, they think about a reconciliation.

Milwaukee was the second city in the United States to establish a court of reconciliation. (Cincinnati was first.) In Milwaukee 60 per cent of all divorce cases filed never go any farther than filing. Much of this record is credited to the conciliation efforts of their own courts. This is a necessary part of the machinery of modern social life. One thing we can do is to see that divorce isn't merely a police court procedure with a chute there like they have at the packing house—once a sheep gets in, he goes right on to slaughter. No one should be allowed to get a divorce without having submitted the situation to counselors or a court of conciliation or a clinic such as a dozen cities now have, because most divorces are unnecessary and undesirable, and both parties are worse off afterward than they were before. Divorces can be prevented with a moderate amount of effort—sometimes just a little delay.

How are we going to prepare the children for divorce? Frankly, I don't know. It is an assignment I used to give my students, most of whom were mature, married persons, graduate students. I asked, "If you had to get a divorce, how would you prepare the children for it?" Nobody ever gave me an intelligent answer.

My brother directed an agricultural school in Central America, and they had great difficulty in making the students face up to examination questions. In one case they asked the student, "You want to grow pineapples for the market; what kind of soil and climate would you select?" The student simply writes down, "I do not want to grow pineapples for the market," and he passes the paper back. That is all he has to say. Some of my students come back the same way. They said, "I can't imagine myself getting a divorce. I have nothing to say on this subject."

It is important to avoid making the divorce an open scandal. The lawyers are too ready to do that, especially in a contested case, where they hope to get a better settlement by making it appear that the man is a brute. You can't trust what the newspapers say. Lawyers may pile up everything they can to make a case, and the newspapers may then pick out one item that will make a good story, but it may give a very inadequate picture of the real cause of the divorce.

I remember a case in San Francisco where a newspaper said the wife charged that on cold nights her husband would make her go to bed first, and after she got a spot warm he would make her move over on the cold side of the bed and he would get into the warm spot. Probably there were more reasons than that. If that was all, any counselor could have solved that problem. He could have bought a hot water bottle for them.

One problem is to avoid having the children poisoned against their own father. He may not be all that he ought to be, and you don't want to try to whitewash him, but it isn't good for them or anybody else if they go through life with the wrong kind of pattern. Publicity and discussion should be no worse than is absolutely unavoidable, because of the harm it will do to the children.

Generally it is thought that children shouldn't have a divided home. Sometimes a child is given to the father for six months of a year and to the mother for the other six. In that case he has no home. The general verdict of the people who are familiar with this field is that the child should have one home and know definitely that it is his home. He may spend eleven months of the year out of his home, but for the sake of security and his own feeling of permanence, of not being uprooted, there should be one place that he feels is his home. We all need that.

The matter of visitation rights is, of course, a difficult one. It is one that mothers particularly resent. The father takes the children out on Sundays and tries to bribe them or buy their loyalty by spending more money on them than his wife does the rest of the week. She complains that when they come back their discipline is shot to pieces. Or if the father visits them in the home, the wife gets out while he spends the evening with them. He cross-examines the children carefully, and after the mother returns the little girl says, "Mother, Daddy asked if there were any empty beer cans in the kitchen. Do we have any empty beer cans in the kitchen?" There isn't anything good about this.

The wife's readjustment after the divorce is one of the points at which we surely can give help. She experiences serious damage to her ego. The husband has the same problem, although he doesn't feel it perhaps quite so seriously because, as I say, marriage means more to the wife than it does to the husband. What is she going to do? How is she going to get along? She doesn't get enough alimony to live on. In most cases she has to go out and take a job. This is good for her but hard on the children.

We haven't paid enough attention to the question of whether the woman should remarry the husband she has recently divorced. In many cases that is the most satisfactory thing to do. I published a study many years ago of two hundred cases in which two persons who got a divorce later remarried each other. Sometimes one or both had been through one, two, three, or four other marriages in the meantime, but they finally came back to their "first love." In half the cases those remarriages turned out well, perhaps as well as they would have done with anybody else they might have married. The statistical average of ordinary marriage after a divorce shows that it is only half as successful as first marriage. The way should be kept open, but it should be made clear that remarriage without thorough preparation is undesirable. It shouldn't be considered until the causes of the first difficulty have been analyzed adequately and removed, or at least identified so that they won't cause the same difficulty again. There's where the clergymen and others might come in. The wife needs to profit by her first failure in order to succeed the second time, and she should have counseling for that purpose. The husband also should receive counseling help before remarriage is considered.

The need of these women for social life after divorce is a serious problem in large cities. Divorcees tend to congregate in the urban areas, of course. They gather in the apartment houses and lead very unhappy lives. In many instances there are no children, but they find it difficult to have a normal social life. Many times they feel so inferior, at least unconsciously, that they are a little hesitant about going out to church and other affairs. There isn't much satisfaction for unattached women in social life in a city. They are objects of suspicion in many cases. They have feelings of unworth, feelings that people don't trust them. Their old friends keep away.

Social life is based on married couples, and when husband and wife break up there isn't any place for them in their old circle. The wives in the circle are particularly alert to make sure that a divorced woman isn't welcomed too enthusiastically by their husbands. Such women have a difficult time. That is one reason why an organization such as Parents Without Partners has been successful. However, it reaches mostly those who are parents, and half the divorced women have no children. They get into the most difficulty, I suppose, trying to find a social life while drifting around on the outskirts. More such organizations are perhaps needed.

This is one of the points at which every church might well take stock of what it has to offer. A church in Los Angeles started a sort of Parents Without Partners enterprise, but the women without children and the unmarried women and men descended on them almost immediately. They said, "This is discrimination—you can't do this to us. We are entitled to a little consideration, too." Finally they changed the name to The Unattached Group or something of the sort. Now anybody who isn't married can come, whether they ever have been married or ever expected to be. The club is serving a valuable purpose. We need more like it.

One of the most unpleasant problems in this area is the attempted exploitation of the divorcee, and to some extent also of the widow and the single woman. The stories divorcees tell are enough to shake one's faith in human nature. They are almost immediately disillusioned about the integrity of the men around them. One woman complained that as soon as she got her divorce, even before they left the courtroom, her attorney, who was an old friend of the family, leaned over and said, "I am glad I have your telephone number. I'll be wanting to see a good deal of you now."

Divorcees are continually victimized; and because of the large number of them, they represent a serious problem. They haven't had any preparation for this problem. Many of them married early. They never learned how to get along in a world of exploitative men. We need to deal with this more frankly in the education of young people. Divorcees are frequently shocked and hurt and need some specific help in learning how to manage. They complain continually that they are propositioned on the first date or at least never later than the second date. Many of them declare, "I never get a third date with any man—the second date is the end." Others get into tragic difficulties. It is one of the matters which we ought to stop joking about and take more seriously and give the women some practical help.

For many years we have had a class at the American Institute of Family Relations called "New Horizons for Widows and Divorcees" where we help these women make readjustments. Most of those that come are divorcees. They demand specific assistance, not generalities. We have made some effort to learn from those who succeed in getting along with the wolves, who I am sure are no more numerous in Los Angeles than in other urban centers, how they manage and what they recommend. What do you do when you are propositioned? We find that they consider this subject very profitable for discussion. They contribute their own experiences, and a half-dozen points have emerged which they think should be passed along.

The first thing, of course, is to be prepared ahead of time, say these divorcees and widows. This is equally true with the teen-age girl on a date. Have a plan in advance, just as a chess player does, as to what you are going to do and how you are going to do it. Don't drift along and end up parked in a car on a dark road. Beyond this plan in advance, how are you going to meet each possible situation? This applies equally, as I say, to the high school girl or the college girl. The high school age is the dangerous age, of course, for both sexes. If they get through that successfully, they probably will get through college without sexual disaster. Major breakdown is in the high school years.

In the second place, it's important to dissociate the action from the man. Here is a man the girl would like to date again. Rather than simply slapping his face and humiliating him so that he will never come back, her attitude can be: "I like you, but I don't like your approach." She can usually set the tone at the beginning. It is easy for her to make her stand clear, directly or indirectly, before they start out. He is entirely in the dark as to what she expects. Many of these fellows think she should be delighted to have him proposition her. On the other hand, many think they are not real men unless they do. They would be astounded and frightened if the girl accepted the proposition.

She will avoid much trouble if she will simply make her position clear in advance.

The third point, they tell us, is to follow the clue of his approach in giving an answer. They get propositioned in all sorts of ways: sometimes in crude and brutal ways, sometimes pseudo-romantic, sometimes flippant, sometimes serious, sometimes argumentative. If he makes a flippant proposition, answer it flippantly. If he makes a pseudo-romantic approach the girl might say: "My, you make that sound like such a wonderful experience. It is the sort of thing a girl would want to last for a lifetime. It would certainly be very unsatisfactory to have just a start in such a wonderful world and have it cut short. If it were a lifetime, it would certainly sound like a very desirable idea." If he makes it appear that the whole conversation is just a sort of joke, she can laugh it off as a joke and get into some other action. If she follows his keynote, she will avoid some complications.

Usually it isn't worthwhile, they tell me, to get into an argument on this subject. On the other hand, if he is a reasonable sort of a person and has been reading the wrong kind of literature—of which we get far too much from some psychiatrists and other sources that ought to know better—and if she is well-informed, she can always beat him at his own game.

L. A. Kirkendall made many studies of this, especially among young men. He asked the boys about the girls they went with, in this matter of sexual relations. He says the boys tell him that the girls they are afraid of are those that have all the answers. If the girl hasn't any answer, they can beat her. But when they meet a girl who knows more than they do and can answer every suggestion they put forward by making it appear entirely foolish, unscientific, or out of date, they change the conversation right away.

We have a pamphlet at the American Institute of Family Relations called, "Are Virgins Out of Date?" which tells young women how to meet all these arguments. The pastor of a church in Los Angeles bought two thousand copies. He said, "This is exactly what we want the girls in this community to have. We are going to spread it everywhere." Another of our pamphlets, "Building Sex into Your Life," has helped young men to recognize the scientific basis of continence and chastity. The New Jersey Board of Health gets five thousand at a time, and it is widely used in high schools and colleges. Material like this gives the woman scientific background, together with whatever spiritual resources she may have, to deal with these fellows who are not easily discouraged. She can beat them at their own game.

Next, my clients advise, "Say no as if you meant it." Many of them reply when they are propositioned, "Why, of course not. Why on earth should I?" and then turn the subject to something else.

The final trump card, so to speak, is—after making the situation crystal clear—to get into another line of discussion or turn to something else right away so that the issue doesn't drag on. If that is done, there won't be many difficulties the woman can't handle.

In the marriage interrupted by travel, military service, and the like, the family must be kept together sentimentally, spiritually, and emotionally. That can be helped by the father's frequent writing to the children as well as to the mother. He can afford to take a considerable amount of time for this purpose. The mother, on the other hand, wants to be careful not to make the father out as a sort of a demigod when he is not there (he can't live up to it when he comes back) or to use him as a sort of absentee whipping boy, saying, "It would hurt your father's feelings," or "You would break your father's heart." It is up to her to handle those problems and not try to use the father's image to beat the youngsters into subjection. She should, however, say, "Your father and I feel that this is the way it ought to be done," and be firm about it. She can make abundant use of the family council so that the youngsters have a chance to express their own opinions.

The family council should be part of every home. Of course we don't want many like the one in which the father said: "Look here, Son, if you want to continue to take part in our family council you will have to learn to keep your mouth shut the same as I do."

One of the problems in these cases of the absent father is that the wife has had to exercise all authority for months or perhaps several years. Unconsciously she is reluctant to give it up when the husband comes back. She may have the feeling: "I have been deciding for a long time how to spend the money. I guess I can keep on doing it."

Then there is the problem of the unmarried mother. We have a quarter of a million each year in America. This is not at all a monopoly of women, for every child of an unmarried mother also has an unmarried father. He is the forgotten man in this picture. There is very little available on the subject. We need research on it, and we need to do more with the men.

There's the problem of a forced marriage. There's the problem of whether the man on whom the girl is putting the finger actually is the father, which in many cases is not true. Often the girl doesn't know who the father is. I have known cases where the girl said: "I really don't know who the father is. I was out with a number of fellows, and we all got dead drunk. I woke up the next morning, and I don't know who had been with me. It might have been anybody at all."

Other countries have faced this difficulty. In the Soviet Union, I understand, the whole history of every man in the community is known. He gets his income from the state, and it is a matter of record. If the girl says that it might have been one of several, they simply look up the records. The man who has the highest income is made ex officio father because he can do more for the child by having more money. In the Scandinavian countries, I am told, it becomes a syndicate. The girl says, "It might have been any one of several." The court says, "If that's the case, we'll just establish that fact, and each of them is in part responsible." If there are four of them, each contributes 25 per cent to the support of the child. It might be his, and they are not going to quibble over a technicality.

The use of a blood test is always brought up, but it doesn't prove who is the father. It may prove that a man could not have been the father. Otherwise, he might have been.

Finally, there is the problem of the stepchild or adopted child. There are two or three points that come up continually in our experience. In the first place, if the man has children he is trying to find a mother for them. They need a mother, and he marries a wife for the purpose of taking care of the children. There are other reasons, but she is made to feel that her job now is to take care of the children. The children don't feel the same about it. They say to her: "You can't boss us around. You are not our mother."

Here again the family council is invaluable, but the new mother should insist that the children's father handle the discipline as far as possible. Apart from that, she can try to be a sort of big sister, helping them and seeing that they all have allowances so they don't have to come to her for money. She doesn't try to exercise unjustifiably an authority or discipline which they feel she isn't entitled to. They work together.

Traditionally, the stepmother is the one who makes trouble. However, I think the figures show that the stepfather is the real offender, if there is real offense. He makes more difficulty, especially in the area of incest. Stepfathers may take advantage of adolescent stepdaughters. The stepmother has much to answer for, but on ten times as many occasions she is a blessing to all. The stepfather is more likely to be the offender, and the offense is much more serious than in the case of the stepmother, who is simply trying to establish herself with children who resent her. However, this fact should not obscure the general case, that he too is a blessing to all.

12

The Man in the Home

The greatest difference in the behavior of men and women is the greater aggressiveness of the male. Man is more aggressive in his work, in his play, in his home, in his business, in his politics, in his church and religious activities. This greater aggressiveness goes back to a time when if the male couldn't fight to defend his family the whole group would be exterminated. Some of those able to fight to protect themselves survived and left descendants. Man still follows this ancient pattern, frequently in ways that are harmful; but it is inevitably present in the normal male. We have to recognize that this aggressiveness is ingrained and is going to continue to be present.

It is time to ask ourselves more carefully how we can develop boys to be real men and girls to be real women. We have allowed the aggressiveness of the male to be perverted too often into exploiting women rather than protecting them. On the other hand, too many women have tried to be second-rate men instead of first-rate women and have outdone the man in aggressiveness. If she is brought up that way by her mother, this aggressiveness of the female interferes seriously with her likelihood of marriage, her likelihood of happiness if she does marry, and particularly in the likelihood that she can raise her boys to be successful men and girls to be good women. Too many boys grow up unwilling to accept responsibility because they never were allowed to do so in their own home. The common complaint is that it is hard to find men who have initiative, self-reliance, self-control, and willingness to accept responsibility. They fail to recognize the balance between privileges and responsibilities. What we like to think of as the traditonal American virtues in the male are often hard to find nowadays.

Apart from failure in marriage and failure in citizenship, we are producing an intolerable crop of males with homosexual tendencies. We have six million, according to the best estimates that can be made. I want to take time to discuss that problem because it is another of those that we try to brush under the rug. We don't like to face these persons or talk about them; we don't like to believe that we could have a responsibility. We like to think: After all, they are not our kind of people. We don't have anything to do with them, and the best way is to ignore them. Five or six million definitely homosexual men in the population are five or six million too many. Even one is too many. We are now gaining in understanding, I think, although this is still one of the most controversial and uncertain areas in the entire range of human biology and behavior. We are getting a better idea of the causes of homosexuality, the ways it can be prevented, the ways it can be cured, and of the difficulty and damage that it produces.

The presence of homosexuals has been noted all through history. The Bible has references to them. But, at present in the United States and in other nations, they are becoming more aggressive and beginning to demand that they be recognized as just as good as anybody else and be treated as such. They have an international organization that claims to include thirty countries. In the United States they have at least three national organizations and probably many local ones. Three have their headquarters in California, two of them for men and one for women. They publish national magazines and other literature which may be found on the newsstands. It is unbelievable how aggressive they have become, how widespread their activities are. They are no longer on the defensive. They are on the offensive, and they are going to become more aggressive.

These organizations which are prepared to demand their "rights" are developing a platform which consists of a number of planks. I want to present these because I think we need to know what is going on.

1. In the first place, they claim that any homosexual, male or female, should be allowed to serve his or her country in any branch of its armed forces. They say that discrimination against them must stop.

2. Second, they say that homosexuals should be qualified for any government job, whether it is a so-called sensitive job or not. Terrible damage can be done by the presence of homosexuals in an area like the State Department because of their susceptibility to blackmail. If these programs were carried out, there wouldn't be any basis for blackmail.

3. Third, they claim that "marriages" between homosexual members or persons of the same sex should be recognized by law. This would include tax exemption, husband and wife ownership of property, and other advantages, regardless of whether the "wife" is a male or a female.

4. Fourth, they say that homosexual couples should be allowed to adopt children if they meet the usual standards applied to intersexual couples.

5. Fifth, they claim that bans on the representation of homosexual life in films and television and elsewhere should be eliminated. Any artistic treatment of homosexuality and homosexual behavior should be subject merely to the same general criteria of good taste that are now applied to heterosexual relationships and personalities.

6. Sixth, homosexual love and marriage should be fully, frankly, and specifically accepted by the churches. The invert should be received, subject only to the same criteria that apply to any other person.

7. Seventh, they claim that homosexuals should be permitted to wear the clothing appropriate to their natures and not to their legal sex, just as heterosexuals are permitted to wear clothing appropriate to theirs. Decisions on such matters as the

use of make-up, perfume, hair styles, and the like should be left entirely with the individual.

8. Eighth, they say that the homosexual press should be allowed freedom equal to that of the heterosexual press. For example, if a heterosexual magazine is permitted to feature female nudes and the like, the homosexual magazine should be permitted to do the same for males. If intersexual pen pals and lonely heart clubs are permitted to exist, homosexual groups should be allowed to advertise and build up clientele.

9. And in the ninth place, they argue that homosexuals should have the same freedom to make romantic sexual advances and overtures in the presence of their own sex that others now have between the two sexes.

That will give you an idea of the propaganda of these organizations. The most active and largest is a society called "One," with headquarters in Los Angeles. It gets out a monthly magazine called *One* which is widely circulated. The second national organization, The Mattachine Society, started in Los Angeles, and is still listed in the telephone directory there. They moved to San Francisco not long ago. The third, a woman's organization called the "Daughters of Bilitis," has its headquarters in San Francisco.

We have to face up to this and ask ourselves whether we are willing to accept it. It is a ruinous sort of thing. We should be prepared, in the first place, to protect boys against it. By ignoring it we have allowed them to be exploited unknowingly. In the second place, we should be prepared to deal with the arguments. I am not going into those, except to make one point. Frequently we are assured: "These folks are more to be pitied than censured. They can't help it. They damage themselves, but they don't damage the rest of us. Leave them alone and let them sink in their own iniquities." Obviously homosexuality can exist only by a continual supply of new recruits. There is a continuous exploitation of boys for that purpose.

How are we going to prevent homosexuality in the first place? That is the important thing. With those in the earlier stages, especially adolescents, it isn't too difficult by energetic, intelligent, well-directed, well-informed counseling to redirect them and get them out of their difficulties. With the more hardened specimen, the redirection, the re-education, is difficult. In the past many well-informed persons have alleged that there is no case on record in which a real homosexual has been changed back. It is now evident that that is by no means the fact. We have adequate records from a variety of sources showing that, in principle, any homosexual who wants to be changed can be changed by counseling. It is one of the jobs that most of us would just as soon not have, but it can be done.

We will have to make it clear that anybody who is a homosexual is so from choice. We have heard the old argument that they were born that way and that it is as natural for them to be homosexual and us to be heterosexual as it is for you to have brown eyes and me to have blue eyes. If biological determination is a matter of importance, it is extremely rare. As a biologist myself, I started out with the supposition that this was mostly a constitutional problem. Evidence forced me to believe that it rarely is.

Homosexuals originate in their homes. They are the product of badly organized fathers and badly organized mothers. Any well-organized home will not produce homosexual boys. Real homosexuality is not, as the psychologist and psychoanalyst have often assured us, a factor in all personalities—that anybody can be homosexual, and we all have that tendency. I don't think there is any basis for that. The boy who becomes a homosexual or who can be exploited grows up in a home where his father was a weakling or definitely hostile.

Absence of the father doesn't seem to be a factor, certainly not an important one. It is the father who is present and whom the boy despises: "If that's what a man is like, just include me out. I certainly don't want to be a man if men are like my father. My mother is the one who runs things around here; she is the one who gets things done. She's the one who lays down the law. That's good enough for me. I'm going to be like her."

So the relation of the father and mother to each other is the decisive factor. If the father and mother love each other, have a warm relationship with each other, if the mother is not an aggressive, overpossessive "mom" who doesn't get enough love from her husband and tries to take it out on her son, the boy is going to get along all right.

We have to produce more successful, strong men in order to prevent having their wives step in and take their places. In most cases the wife doesn't want to be the boss of the home. She is forced to because her husband is a weakling. We have to produce more masculine fathers and fewer masculine mothers, otherwise the children of both sexes, but particularly the boys, are going to pay a terrible penalty for the unsuccessful marriage of their parents. We can't afford to drift any longer in this situation. As parents we can't afford to refuse the responsibility for it. It is definitely our responsibility, and we have to prepare the whole educational system—home, church, school, and community organizations—to deal with it. There are many other reasons for reorganizing this educational system to produce more successful men. I want to enumerate briefly some of the changes that are needed.

1. We must have the father on the job as a father. For a couple of decades (it is somewhat past now) there was a trend in the literature on this subject to assure everybody that the father and mother must be equal in the home. In the opinion of these writers—who were mostly frustrated women—the father should do his own work downtown and then come home and do half the mother's work in the home. There shouldn't be any distinctions on the basis of sex. In such cases the children didn't have any father; they had a mother and an assistant mother. They grew up without understanding what fathers are like, what fathers are for, what the difference is, why anybody should have a father and mother. One was enough!

2. In the second place, we need more masculine patterns in community organizations—Boy Scouts, YMCA groups, and summer camps. We need more church groups and Sunday school

classes led by strong men rather than women. Women have done a wonderful job in many ways, but I think we should lean over backward in the present crisis to make sure that our classes for boys are taught by strong young men, even from the earliest ages.

3. In the third place, we face the serious problem of the unfair competition which exists throughout our coeducational school system. No system has all the advantages and no possible drawbacks, but the coeducational system seems, almost inescapably, to put boys and girls of the same age in the same class. When they enter the first grade at the age of six, boys and girls are associating from the very beginning on the basis of calendar age, which has little to do with emotional maturity and real social adjustment age. When they enter the first grade at six, the girls are already a year or more matured than the boys. By the time they get into senior high school, the girls are two or three years ahead of the boys in their social and emotional maturity. In addition to that, the boys and girls are not co-operating; they are competing against each other.

A farm family is the only really normal biological unit left in this country, and there are not many of them. In California one family in every thirteen now lives on the farm; twelve of them are city families. Probably in most of the southern states the proportion is a little higher than that, but I doubt if there's any state in the union where more than 25 or 30 per cent of the families live on the farm. We have moved the family off the farm to the city, and to a considerable extent we have destroyed it as a normal educational agency. In the old days children grew up and got their education by growing up, getting it right in the home. They learned to do by doing. In the Colonial period there were few schools. Children grew up on the farm and took part in the activities around them. The farm family was a co-operative unit—one for all and all for one. All co-operated for the success of the family and the success of the farm.

The minute you move the family into the city, that educational function is largely destroyed. In the first place, the father is taken out of the home. If he is like most of us, he rushes away as quickly as he gets up in the morning and gets breakfast. Then he gets home at night just about in time to help put the children to bed if they are small, or sit up and wait for them to come in if they are a little older. They say the parents of an adolescent spend half their time wondering how he is going to turn out and the other half wondering when he is going to turn in. In either case, they don't have a very close relationship with him. So we take the father out of the home. His work isn't in the home; it is in some other part of the city, frequently in an adjoining city. Next we take the mother out of the home, too, and in any case we take the children out of the home. There is nothing for them to do in the home, nobody for them to play with. They get under their mother's feet and on her nerves, so we take them out as quickly as we can. We put them in kindergarten at five, if there is one. If there's a nursery school we put them in at three and a half.

When I made that remark while speaking in Topeka, my cousin, who runs a nursery school there, said, "Oh, you Californians are always so far behind the times. We take them at twelve months!" It isn't much of an exaggeration to say that almost before a child is weaned he is taken away from his home and put into a herd, biologically speaking—that is, the little group of boys and girls his own age, with whom he then goes on from year to year, each learning by trial and error from the ignorance of the others, for none of them knows any more than the rest of the herd.

The boys are continually competing against girls who are too mature for them. They continue competing from the first grade on—competing for marks, competing for teacher's favor, competing for election to class offices—the girls beating the boys because they are more mature. In high school, when they are beginning to date, the boys are associating with girls who are much too mature for them, and both of them are dissatisfied. It is extremely unfortunate that we have to organize social life on the basis of classes. Still, it is not easy to do anything else. Ideally, the girls in the freshman class shouldn't be going with the boys in the freshman class, who are still back in the early Boy Scout period. They should be going with boys in the senior class, who are old enough to make life interesting for them. Girls in the senior class shouldn't be wasting time on the high school boys at all. Probably they should be going with the young men in the Junior Chamber of Commerce and the 20–30 Club downtown who are out in business and prepared to talk business to them.

I made that remark once in a meeting of high school administrators in Los Angeles. I thought I was being facetious, but, as often happens, I wasn't facetious enough because a vice-principal got up with a hard look and said: "That doesn't work; we tried it."

"Well," I said, "I like to see things tried. That is the way we find out. What happened?"

"Why," she said, "in our high school we dated the senior boys and the freshman girls, and it was a tremendous success. Then we found we had to date the senior girls with the freshman boys, and they weren't satisfied."

I am not suggesting that we ought to give up coeducation. It has many advantages, and we are certainly not going to abandon it. I am merely pointing out that, with all its advantages, it has at least one disadvantage that is sometimes overlooked, in that it does not particularly encourage the development of some of the most desirable masculine qualities in boys, and that we have not made sufficient effort to offset this handicap.

There's no easy solution. I suggest that the church can help to take up the slack here. We have to make certain that the boys are not continually associated with girls who are more mature and who unconsciously slip into a sort of a maternal role, making all the decisions and letting the boys just go along and say, "Yep, that looks all right to me," thereby becoming good candidates for "yes, my dear" husbands later on. We have to help boys develop more initiative in dealing with the other sex in this adolescent period, to develop self-confidence and avoid feelings of inferiority and dependence on the women, to overcome, as far as possible, the deep-seated fear of the female sex that every man has deep down inside of him, because these feelings of inadequacy and fear of the female sex are often the basis for exploitation of the female. A boy thinks they never treated him properly, so he will do them as much damage as possible!

We'll have to prevent premature sexual experiences by more careful education. We must build up more understanding of the psychological differences between the sexes that are almost completely ignored in the educational system, and develop a feeling of responsibility. The place to start that, of course, is in the home.

It is astounding and tragic to read the figures telling how little responsibility young people in the city home have. A study of freshmen girls was made in the Home Economics Department at Ohio State University. We'll assume the average age was eighteen, which is old enough not only to marry legally but to marry legally without the consent of parents. Fifty per cent of those girls had never had an allowance, had never learned to handle money at all, although within a few years they were going to be made responsible for handling family finances. I wouldn't be surprised if they got into difficulties for lack of experience. Twenty-five per cent of the girls had never even washed a dish. Their mothers thought they were too good for that sort of thing. Mother washed all the dishes herself. They weren't the families who had hired help. The daughter was just brought up as a parasite. She mustn't spoil her fingernails by getting them in the dishpan.

Now I don't think anybody can be educated successfully who hasn't learned how to wash dishes. Since my wife and I have no daughters, only four sons, our boys weren't brought up with any foolish ideas about certain things being women's work and not suitable for a man. In due time they were all in the armed forces. They didn't have to be thrown out with a neuro-psychiatric discharge because they couldn't accept the jobs assigned to them in kitchen police!

Boys aren't brought up to accept responsibility. They are not given any chores. People ask, "What chores can a boy do in the city?" It is astonishing how many you can find if you sit down at the family council and make a list of all the things that have to be done and then sort them out. The family council again is the way to meet this problem to a very large extent, because it develops initiative, resourcefulness, a willingness to accept responsibility, and the recognition that life is a balance between privileges and responsibilities. Youngsters should learn that there's no responsibility that doesn't have some privilege; there's no privilege that doesn't have some responsibility; that the basis of good citizenship in the home, in marriage, in politics, or anywhere else is to recognize that responsiblities and privileges go together.

One of the responsibilities we all have, if we are motivated at all by the Christian ethic, is to recognize that we have some responsibility for seeing that people less privileged than ourselves are not too much underprivileged. It is easy for the older to take advantage of the younger in the home, for example. In a family with several children, the older children ought at least to learn to respect the rights of the younger child and not run over him. The younger child should learn that because he is living in a home where justice prevails he doesn't have to fight all the time to get his rights.

Chores are one of the best educational features of a youngster's life. We will have to find more of them, and the way to do it is to deprive ourselves. We need to make more sacrifices for our children. Many sacrifices we make shouldn't be made, but we should sacrifice the privilege of doing some of the work around the home so that the children can have a fair chance to do it and thereby learn what life is like. I sometimes think, purely ideally, that the parents shouldn't do anything around the home that the children could do fairly well, and that is particularly true of the mother. She sometimes makes a slave of herself and lets both the boys and girls be parasites. They should take over the work a little more each year, so that by the time the girls are in high school they should be doing most of the work of the home. The mother would have that much more time free to take more part in the work of the church and the community and be preparing herself for the great change after the children leave home.

If we are going to help boys grow up to be real men, I suggest the yardstick of self-knowledge, self-control, and unselfishness. There are books written on emotional maturity, but they boil down, for my purpose, to the above yardstick. In all three areas, the adult stands at the opposite pole from the infant.

We are going to have to help boys avoid destructive habits based on infantile patterns. The most conspicuous is alcoholism, which is a means of seeking to escape from adult responsibilities—largely that, at least. Roger Williams, a famous biochemist, has brought out evidence that in some people alcoholism is really an allergy. The individual just can't take alcohol, just as some other people can't take tomatoes or eggs. But by and large it represents an attempt to avoid responsibility, to escape from unpleasant things, just as a child does. Alcoholism is one of the serious problems associated mainly with failure to bring up boys to be real men and girls to be real women.

Another, according to psychoanalysts—I think here maybe they have something—is the use of tobacco. When the infant was unhappy, he would turn to the mother's breast. By clamping on to that he would forget his troubles and begin to feel better. The rest of his life, every time he feels the same way he pulls on a cigarette. That, in his mouth, is the symbolical substitute for the mother's nipple. He turns to it any time he feels a little frustrated and irritable, just as he did in earlier life when he would call for the bottle or the nipple at the end of the bottle.

Can we develop now the co-operative patterns that are so necessary in life? Can we avoid both the competitive patterns between the sexes which are so destructive in marriage, and on the other hand the overdependent patterns which grow up when mother forces on the boy the love which should be going to the boy's father? If so, we will not only straighten out our married life in the next generation by producing a better crop of husbands, but we'll avoid the production in each generation of five or six million homosexuals who are a serious menace to the entire fabric of our culture.